PSYCHOLOGY OF......
HORROR VILLIANS, SURVIVORS, AND VICTIMS.

Vol. 1

Movie Edition

By:

S.L. Yarbrough

First Printing, 2021

ISBN: 979-8-2015-0939-2

Library of Congress Cataloging-in-Publication Data

LCCN: TX0009062367

Cover designed by GetCovers©

Sign up for newsletter **www.slyarbrough.com**[1]

Follow on twitter @SlYarbrough

Instagram @slyarbrough @writereadpublish

To my husband, who has been by my side through this entire process, and my children who have always been supportive and my inspiration.

Disclaimers

All evaluations are done by research of film, written background in books or internet. The author is expressing her opinions regarding the characters motives, mental status, and background. The films used may not be canon as some deviate from the books.

Disclaimer: Even though all characters in this book and true crime stories have criminal behavior and psychological disorders, having any
of these disorders does not mean the individual will commit murder.

Copyright Disclaimer for the use of the characters is under section 107 of the Copyright Act of 1976, allowance is made for "fair use" for purposes such as criticism, comment, news reporting, teaching, scholarship, education, and research.

Fair use is a use permitted by copyright statute that might otherwise be infringing.

**PSYCHOLOGY OF...HORROR VILLIANS, SURVIVORS, AND VICTIMS.
MOVIE EDITION VOL. I**

Coming soon

Horror Villains, Survivors, and Victims Vol. II Movie Edition

Horror Villains, Survivors, and Victims Vol. III TV Edition

Thriller Villains, Survivors, and Victims Vol. IV Movie Edition

Thriller Villains, Survivors, and Victims Vol. V TV Edition

Sci-fi Villains, Survivors, and Victims Vol. VI Movie Edition

Sci-fi Villains, Survivors, and Victims Vol. VII TV Edition

Fantasy Villains, Survivors, and Victims Vol. VIII Movie Edition

Fantasy Villains, Survivors, and Victims Vol. IX TV Edition

Drama Villains, Survivors, and Victims Vol. X Movie Edition

Drama Villains, Survivors, and Victims Vol. XI TV Edition

Comedy Villains Vol. XII Movie Edition

Comedy Villains Vol. XIII TV Edition

Comic Villains and Anti-Heroes Vol. XIV Movie Edition

Comic Villains and Anti-Heroes Vol. XV TV Edition

Comic Heroes Vol. XVI Movie Edition

Comic Heroes Vol. XVII TV Edition

Action Movie Edition Vol. XVIII

Action TV Edition Vol. XIX

Foreign Films Vol. XX

Coming of Age 80s Edition

Coming of Age 90s Edition

Coming of Age 2000s+ Edition

Black Cinema 70s Edition

Black Cinema 80s Edition

Black Cinema 90s Edition

Black Cinema 2000s+ Edition

Black Director's Edition

Table of Contents

Split: Casey Cooke
Nightmare on Elm St: Nancy Thompson, Alice Johnson, Maggie, Tracy, and Doc.
Frankenstein Unbound: Dr. Buchanan

Psychopath vs Sociopath

What is the difference between a Psychopath and a Sociopath? These terms have been used interchangeably, but there are differences. Robert Hare created the first mental health tool to detect psychopathology.

The PCL-R provides criminologists, law enforcement, and the courts a way to check the mental stability of criminals. The ability to differentiate between psychopaths and other mental disorders.

The PCL-R uses twenty traits. Each of these is given a score of 0,1, or 2. If the score is 30 or higher, an individual can be diagnosed with psychopathy. Normal noncriminal individuals will have an average score of 5. Criminals with no psychopathy will score around 22 (Life Explores, 2021).

Listed below are the fundamental differences between the two.

Moral Awareness

Psychopaths: Have no sense of right and wrong, they lack a conscience, and have a lack of moral insight.

Sociopaths: Have a sense of right and wrong but feel unconstrained by morality.

Emotions

Psychopaths: Incapable of emotion or empathy for others.

Sociopaths: Capable of emotion but has limited capacity for empathy.

Relationships

Psychopaths: Unable to form emotional bonds with others.

Sociopaths: Able to form emotional bonds with certain individuals under certain circumstances.

Outward Appearance

Psychopaths: They will give the appearance of someone who is successful, intelligent, charming, composed, sincere, and trustworthy.

Sociopaths: They are usually irritable, restless, impatient, and hot-tempered.

Social Skills

Psychopaths: They are manipulative, deceitful, narcissistic, predatory, and skilled at playing roles.

Sociopaths: They are antisocial, unsophisticated, heedless, and get what is desired by taking it.

Violence

Psychopaths: When acting on their violent tendencies, they are cold-bloodied, premeditated, controlled, symbolic, deliberately cruel, and furtive.

Sociopath: Unlike a Psychopath, they are spontaneous, uncontrolled, reactive, explosive, and flagrant.

Criminal Methods

Psychopaths: Are very detailed in planning, they are secretive, use risk management, and prolonged torture.

Sociopaths: They lack planning, have knee-jerk reactions, confrontational, use speed, and savagery.

Motivation

Psychopaths: Thrive on power, control, exploitation, greed, and revenge.

Sociopaths: Feel a sense of entitlement, are angry, seek revenge, and for recreation.

Examples

Psychopaths: Ted Bundy, Jeffrey Dahmer, John Wayne Gacy **Sociopaths:** "Night Stalker" Richard Ramirez, Lizzie Borden

INTRODUCTION

Welcome to Psychology of...Horror Villains, Survivors, and Victims. I will give insight and review theories which may explain their behaviors. In each section a psychological disorder will be discussed.

At the end of the section true stories will be spotlighted.

Each disorder will have more detailed explanations in the glossary. Every film and character discussed can be found in the index.

I have had an affinity for horror from an early age. Although, the first film that scared me was not a horror film. At four-years-old I went with my parents to see the re-release of Snow White. The transformation scene where the evil queen becomes the witch was frightening to me. The Wizard of Oz was another one, the flying monkeys scared me.

The first real horror film I saw was The Omen. Weekly excursions to the drive-in fueled my horror obsession. Movies such as, Carrie, Phantasm, Friday the 13th, Howling, The Mausoleum, Wolfen, Company of Wolves, Halloween (I could go on and on) formed my love of writing horror.

When I decided to look at the Psychology of Horror Villains, I found death as the common goal of the villain. An aspect which frightens us. For some of the villains, death eludes them. Some return as demented supernatural beings: others have lost their humanity therefore no longer connect with the living.

As human beings, we question our very existence. We know we are alive, but we wonder what happens to us after death. To some, death is a big taboo. We do not want to think about it; let alone face the truth that we all live, and we all die. The inevitably of our deaths may cause severe depression in some and enlightenment in others.

The nature of people is to fear the unknown. Existential Psychology examines our fears of existence. Why are we here? Where did we come from? What is my purpose in life? How can I become successful?

When did you realize your fear of dying? Maybe you have no fear. Maybe you have a curiosity with death. My first fear of death was as a young girl, after my mother read Little Red Riding Hood I cried when I realized the wolf had eaten the grandmother and hunter. I was afraid to die. Why as a young child would I be afraid of dying? Is this fear ingrained in us? The older we get the more we realize our transient nature. According to Daniel Becker M.D., the middle-aged person begins to realize the impending eventuality of death. He refers to this as "existential discourse" which encompasses death, isolation, freedom, and meaning (Becker, 2006).

What differentiates a survivor from a victim? What allows someone to fight instead of freeze in the face of danger? We all find ourselves in a position where we need to either run or face an adversary head on. Not everyone will fight or flee, some will hide. This may be the best solution to survive.

In some instances, your intellect will get you out. For example, to survive Jigsaw, physical strength or stamina did not get you out of the trap. Being able to solve the puzzle helped you survive. Defeating Freddy Krueger took mental strength and stamina.

When analyzing someone the information you have is like puzzle pieces. Sometimes you are given all the right pieces, and everything falls together smoothly. Others will have weird pieces and when put together form a unique puzzle. Sometimes there are missing pieces, and you must figure out what is missing to complete the puzzle. The analysis and backgrounds for some of the villains are full of puzzle pieces. Some are mysteries, all the background pieces to their puzzles are not there. Therefore, the level of detail will be more for some than others.

I will use my background in Psychology, Sociology, Criminal Justice, and Philosophy to analyze each Villain, Survivor, or Victim. I will also bring in Parapsychology theory for those with supernatural elements.

Each section will focus on a psychological disorder and will feature the villain or villains who fit the disorder as well as the survivor(s) or victim(s). I will look at how Psychology views each villain. How has society failed them? How genetics may have been a part of the deviant behavior or behaviors. Is there any positive aspect of the villain's motivation(s)?

As you delve into the Psyche of each, think about how you may have dealt with circumstances which created the deviance. Could you have become the villain in your life story?

How would you react if you were up against one of the Villains? Would you survive or perish?

RESPONSES FROM OTHERS REGARDING DEATH

Are you afraid of death? If so, when did you first fear death? How old were you? *In their own words.

Probably at 18 or so I struggled with fear of death or more so the unknown after. I never let it control me. As time passed, I am more worried about protecting my loved one from death even at my expense. I have accepted that it is out of my control but will fight for survival.

I am not afraid of dying. I watched my family die as I got older and understood it was a release for them. I don't know what I believe but they truly believed there was something after and they were ok. I don't want to die soon but I think when the time comes, I'll accept it.

53. When my mom passed away, nine or so years ago.

When I was 10, I got stuck in an elevator by myself. I literally thought I was going to die in there. (This was way before cellphone. Cellphones has just come out.)

I was about 6 when I feared death, after a close family friend died. I don't really think about dying, but if I do, I probably fear the unknown more than death itself.

24. I'm good now. It's an inevitable part of life.

I don't have a fear of death, it's the way of dying that scares me.

Probably at the age of ten. My grandfather passed and I saw how devastating a death is to those left behind. I wrote about it in my childhood memoir, Walk Don't Run.

Section I

Schizophrenia

Our mind can play dirty tricks on us. Seeing things that are not there. Hearing voices calling to us. Feeling the touch of a breeze when there is none. The annoying feeling of tiny little bugs crawling on your skin.

Any of these sensations can drive someone insane. Imagine, the intensity amplified until you can no longer tell reality from imagination. Once the boundaries are broken, all sense of normality is gone. You are on the cusp of madness.

The Villains in this section have lost all aspects of humanity. At one point in time, they may have been productive members of society but too many stressors caused a mental breakdown. There are some who have always rejected the normalcy of life and pursued violence and terror.

Schizophrenia involves psychosis which affects vision and hearing. People with Schizophrenia do not know if what is going on is real. Hearing voices, seeing things not there, smelling things no one else can or being unable to interact normally with others are some aspects of the disorder.

Schizophrenia is just one disorder within psychotic disorders and the most common. All the Villains in this section have one or more of these symptoms lasting for at least a month.

"They were warned…They are doomed…And on Friday the
13th, nothing will save them."

Friday the 13th (1980)

Pamela Voorhees

Pamela Voorhees Born 1930 (exact date unknown) died June 13, 1979.
Information in this report comes exclusively from the film Friday the 13th
(1980) and biographical information.

Background:

Pamela Voorhees married Elias Voorhees when she was young, estimated age
15. She became pregnant at the age of 16 with their child who she named
Jason. Elias was abusive both mentally and physically. During her pregnancy,
Elias abandons her. She is left alone, no money, destitute. She begins to hear her
unborn child speak to her. This is the first incidence of schizophrenia. She gives
birth, her son is deformed and has intellectual deficits this causes Pamela to be
overprotective of him. The bond between Pamela and Jason was strong. Jason
did not speak much but Pamela could understand him. There was a symbiotic
connection. She was approached about employment at Camp Crystal Lake.
She accepts and moves near the campgrounds.

Inciting Event:

Pamela did not allow Jason out of her sight. He never attended school. Pamela
home schooled him. On the encouragement of her boss, she let Jason go to
camp. Jason was bullied by the other kids and the youth counselors. Jason tried
to escape the bullies but could not. They grabbed him and shoved him in the
lake. He drowned. It was determined the counselors were having sex and were
not watching the children. Pamela was furious. Jason's body was not found.

Murders:

It is suspected that Elias Voorhees was killed by Pamela. Without a body it could not be proven. During her massacre of the camp counselor's, fourteen bodies were discovered. Only one survived and was able to recount what occurred. She survived by beheading Pamela.

Psychological aspect:

Risk factors for developing schizophrenia include genetics, pregnancy, and childbirth complications. During Pamela's pregnancy, she showed symptoms of schizophrenia by believing her unborn child spoke to her. After Jason drowned, she heard Jason telling her to kill. The constant abuse by Elias seems to have triggered her psychosis. The drowning of Jason sent her over the edge causing her to become vengeful. She had no sense of remorse or consequences.

Could Pamela Voorhees have been helped?

Pamela needed a dedicated support system. Where were her parents? Many times, women in abusive relationships feel they have no way to escape. There are numerous cases of women who kill due to battered woman syndrome. Schizophrenia has no cure. There are treatments to help the symptoms.

Pamela would have benefited from an antipsychotic such as olanzapine (Zyprexa). Olanzapine rebalances dopamine and serotonin to improve thinking, mood, and behavior. The medication would reduce episodes of hallucinations. Once her hallucinations were under control, psychotherapy could have begun. Cognitive behavioral therapy would focus on her thinking and behavior. By showing her ways to test reality, she could control the voices.

A supportive home environment allows the person suffering from schizophrenia the stability and encouragement. Having to deal with the stress of caring for Jason, made dealing with her disorder unbearable. She would have to move away from Crystal Lake, then find an assisted living facility where she would get help and support for Jason.

"There's a legend around here. A Killer buried, but not dead. A curse on Crystal Lake, a death curse. Jason Voorhees curse. They say he died as a boy but keeps coming back. Few have seen him and lived. Some have even tried to stop him... No one can. People forget he is down there, waiting..." The *Narrator: Friday the 13th*

Jason Voorhees

Born unknown date in 1946 Undead

Background:

Jason Voorhees a deformed and mentally disabled young boy who lived with his mother near the Campground of Crystal Lake. Due to his disabilities, he was home schooled by his mother. Jason formed an abnormal obedience to his mother. The other children bullied Jason and chased him to the dock where they threw him in. It was assumed that he had drowned, and his body was not found. The camp counselors allowed Jason to be harmed due to having sex instead of watching the campers. Jason somehow did not drown and found a way to stay hidden. He witnessed his mother murder those she felt responsible for his demise and witnessed the beheading of his mother. Seeing the brutality of what his mother did and what happened to her, formed Jason's penchant for violence. Years later after the camp was reopened, an adult Jason came back to Crystal Lake for revenge.

Murders:

It is believed that Jason has killed 161 people. Initially, the victims were late teens to early twenties and appears to murder those who are behaving immorally, such as having premarital sex, drug use, and alcohol use. Later he murders anyone who may be in his way. There have been a few survivors. For someone to survive a confrontation with Jason, you had to find a way to trick him. Ginny Field found Pamela's old sweater and put it on she then tricked Jason, making him believe she was his mother. This was enough time for an attack by Paul.

Another instance where manipulation was used to distract Jason was by young Tommy Jarvis. Tommy used prosthetics and makeup to appear as a young Jason. This distracted him long enough for Tommy to strike him on the head with a machete. The only one who had any chance of defeating Jason was Freddy Krueger.

Philosophical aspect:

It could be argued that Jason was murdering those who deserved it. Was he wrong for wanting to kill those who attempted to kill him and took his mother away from him?

Could Jason Voorhees have been helped?

Jason was victimized at an early age. He already had a deficit with his deformities, his intellectual disabilities, and a mother who was not mentally stable. From an early age, he did not have a proper home life. His mother created a maladaptive family life with her over-protective behavior. He worshipped his mother. He was bullied and had no real interaction with any other children. He never made any friends. He never experienced what being a child was like. Pamela needed to allow Jason to attend a school for children with disabilities. Maybe due to her lack of income, it may not have been a possibility. Jason needed to have at least one friend. Some companionship other than his mother.

After his mother's death, Jason also showed signs of schizophrenia. He could hear his mother speaking to him. It appears that schizophrenia was inherited from his mother.

"I met him fifteen years ago I was told there was nothing left; no reason, no conscience, no understanding in even the most rudimentary sense of life or death, of good or evil, right or wrong. I met this...six-year-old child with this blank, pale, emotionless face, and the blackest eyes-the devil's eyes. I spent eight years trying to reach him, and then another seven trying to keep him locked up because I realized that what was living behind that boy's eyes was purely and simply evil." -Dr. Sam Loomis

Halloween

Michael Myers

Born on October 19, 1957, Undead

Background:

Michael Myers, at 6 years old, murdered his older sister while his parents were at a Halloween party. Judith was supposed to be watching him but was more preoccupied by her boyfriend. Michael spied on his sister and boyfriend through the windows. When they went upstairs to have sex, Michael angry, grabbed a butcher knife and waited until Judith's boyfriend left to murder her. He went upstairs, put on his clown mask, and stabbed her repeatedly.

After murdering his sister, he goes outside still holding the bloody butcher knife as his parents pulled up. He was committed into Smith's Grove Sanitorium. Dr. Loomis was his therapist. While under Dr. Loomis' care, Michael was quiet and sat silently watching. He never caused any trouble. He was a model patient. As the years passed, Dr.

Loomis becomes disturbed by Michael. He could sense something evil within him.

Fifteen years later, Michael escaped the Sanatorium. On his way back to Illinois to kill his younger sister, he murders a mechanic and takes his clothing. He planned his escape during Halloween, so wearing a Halloween mask would not bring any attention to him. He was able to walk around undetected.

Michael's parents died in a car accident while he was committed. His younger sister was adopted by the Strode's, who changed her name to Laurie. Michael went back to his old home to find her. Mr. Strode was the owner of Strode Realty. He listed the Myers home for sale. He had Laurie drop the keys off due to a showing later that day. Michael hiding in the house, watched her leave the keys and recognized her. He follows her everywhere she went. That evening he murders three of Laurie's friends and begins a murder spree.

Laurie fights Michael using a knitting needle to stab him in the neck. Dr. Loomis arrives in time to shoot Michael six times saving Laurie. He gets away and finds Laurie at the hospital. He takes the lives of the doctor and nurses working there. Laurie hides and then finds a way out. Dr. Loomis again assist her in stopping Michael, this time setting him on fire.

Murders:

Michael has killed 121 people (all timelines), his motivation unknown.

The original murder of his sister Judith, stemmed from his feeling of being neglected. Coming back for his younger sister, may have been a sense of unfinished business.

Psychology and parapsychological aspect:

Michael's schizophrenia at such an early age is a rarity. Children are
not often diagnosed with schizophrenia. Usually, they are found to
have conduct disorders. One theory according to the novelization, was Michael was being controlled by the spirit of Enda. A Celtic boy who committed murders on the day of Samhain (present day Halloween) if this was true, supernatural forces were controlling him.

When Michael killed his sister, he put his mask on. He hesitated when attacking Laurie when she pulled his mask off, so he could put it back on. He hid his face behind the mask, as a sense of empowerment. With each murder, Michael grew stronger. He set up his victims in grotesque and creative positions. He rationalized as he stalked and killed.

Could Michael Myers have been helped?

Michael was institutionalized with no success. By the time he was committed it was too late. At the onset of the voices contacting him, he would have needed therapy.

Treatment for a six-year-old, encompasses the cooperation of the parents. Few drugs are approved for young children with schizophrenia. One drug

Aripiprazole treats the symptoms of schizophrenia. It also helps aggressiveness, temper tantrums, and mood changes.

If Enda was truly contacting Michael, a clinical parapsychologist would conduct an assessment, like a behavioral psychologist. During the assessment, the clinician would document Michael's interactions with Enda. The goal would have been to make Michael an unsuitable conduit for Enda. The antipsychotics and therapy could have pushed Enda's control away. Because of the supernatural aspect, his therapist would have to be familiar and believe in alternate possibilities.

"Where we we're going, we don't need eyes to see."-Dr. Weir

Event Horizon

Dr. William Weir (Event Horizon)

Born unknown day 2003 Died 2047

Background:

Dr. William Weir was a scientist and designer of the ship Event Horizon. Dr. Weir's wife committed suicide in their bathtub by cutting her wrist. Her feelings of depression brought on by his frequent time away, was the catalyst to take her own life. Dr. Weir was so immersed in the creation of his ship the Event Horizon nothing else mattered. The death of his wife affected him more deeply than he expected. He became clinically depressed and suffered from PTSD whenever he was in their bathroom, unable to look at the tub without the memory of her bloody body.

The Event Horizon was a scientific anomaly with the ability to travel faster than light. On its first voyage, the ship was lost and did not reappear until seven years later. Dr. Weir was called to investigate the reappearance along with a new crew. While on the ship Dr. Weir began to experience auditory and visual hallucinations. As the hallucinations worsen, Dr. Weir experienced personality changes. He became more disturbed to the point of self-mutilation. The voices he hears command him to protect the ship and to murder the crew.

The remaining crew members also experience hallucinations of their worst fears. These fears cause some of the crew members to commit suicide. To stop Dr. Weir, the captain destroys the drive and separates it from the rest of the ship with him and Dr. Weir inside. This allows three of the crew members to survive.

Murders:

Dr. Weir murdered three of the crew members. He believed the ship wanted him to protect it from the crew.

Could Dr. Weir have been helped?

Dr. Weir needed psychological help after his wife's death. His continued visions of her suicide fueled his schizophrenia. Treatment would have been medication to combat the hallucinations and for PTSD. Use of a SSRI and/or antipsychotic such as fluvoxamine and clozapine. Additionally, group therapy for PTSD where he could have listened to others with similar issues could have helped him cope with his loss.

Omaima Aree Nelson murdered her abusive husband, cut him up, and ate him. Convicted January 12, 1993. She has been denied parole both in 2006 and 2011.

Stacy Castor poisoned her two husbands, then tried to frame her daughter for the murders. She attempted to make it look like her daughter overdosed. Her daughter survived and turned her mother in. She was convicted in 2009 and sentenced to 51 years to life. She died in prison 7 years later.

Katherine Knight a slaughterhouse employee, murdered her boyfriend stabbing him 37 times, skinning him, and chopping him into multiple pieces. Next, she hung his body parts on meat hooks. Unlike the others, Katherine was the abuser. She showed signs of mental instability. She placed her infant daughter on railroad tracks attempting to murder her. Luckily, a neighbor was driving by and saw what was happening. He rushed over and saved the baby. She slit the throat of her ex-husband's puppy and would roam the woods with an axe threatening anyone who would say something. Eventually she was arrested and imprisoned with no chance of parole.

Montgomery County Maryland early 2021, A man driving erratically, hit several vehicles. The incident was caught on camera and the police were called. As the policeman approached, the man grabbed a large tree branch and began hitting him. The Police officer fired his gun twelve times hitting the man. The bullets didn't stop him. He kept advancing threatening. After a few minutes he collapsed, still breathing.

There have been other stories of people refusing to die after being shot, tased, electrocuted, or stabbed multiple times.

Section II
Dissociative Identity Disorder

Sometimes we create persona's which help us get over stage fright. Our new persona will have a different name, way of dress, different speech, and an attitude much unlike our normal demeanor. Once you finish performing, you are back to yourself. Or you may be a writer and there is an area of your imagination you're afraid to let anyone know about, so you create an alias.

Having an alias or stage persona is normal. When your stage persona no longer lives on stage and pours into your everyday life, it becomes another identity.

Dissociative Identity Disorder (DID) previously referred to as Multiple Personality Disorder manifest as separate distinct personalities. Some symptoms experienced by DID patients are amnesia and memory problems. DID patients can have other symptoms such as major depression, anxiety, PTSD, substance abuse, sleep disorders, and self-destructive behavior.

The Villains in this section used at least one of their alternate personalities to commit murder.

"A man cannot destroy savage in him by denying its impulses. The only way to get rid of the temptation is to yield to it." Dr. Henry Jekyll

Jekyll and Hyde

Dr. Henry Jekyll and Mr. Edward Hyde

Born unknown Died unknown

Background:

Dr. Henry Jekyll, a progressive doctor who believed our brain held the key to our behavior. He believed we all had an evil side and a good side with both personalities in competition. With pharmaceuticals the behaviors of the bad personality could be contained. Dr. Jekyll was ridiculed by other physician's due to his unconventional treatments.

He was ashamed of his urges he felt was caused by his evil side. He developed a tonic to suppress his bad behaviors. Instead, he unleashed his alternate self, Mr. Edward Hyde. As Edward Hyde his appearance transformed from a well-groomed, respectful doctor to an unkempt, violent man. As Edward Hyde his violent behaviors and urges were able to be acted upon. Therefore releasing Dr. Jekyll from guilt.

Eventually, Mr. Hyde would appear without the use of the tonic. Dr. Jekyll could not control his evil side anymore.

Murders and violent behavior:

Edward Hyde enjoyed raping and abusing women. He had no remorse in inflicting pain. He threw a man with one hand to his death. He had an abnormal amount of strength. He pushed a young girl out in the street, and she was trampled by a horse. She survived with the help of Dr. Jekyll.

Could Dr. Jekyll have been helped?

Dr. Jekyll understood something was wrong mentally. He attempted to treat himself with medication which went awry. Cognitive Behavioral Therapy would have helped him merge both personalities and find productive ways to deal with his urges.

"As I was going up the stairs, I met a man who wasn't there. He wasn't there again today. I wish, I wish he'd go away." -Malcolm Rivers

Identity

Malcolm Rivers

Born May 10, 1963, Died unknown

Background:

Malcolm Rivers, the only child of Callie Rivers. Callie was a prostitute and had been arrested multiple times for prostitution, petty larceny, and possession of drug paraphernalia. June 11th, 1972, Malcolm was found by the manager abandoned at the Motel. He had been abused and neglected. His mother told him to lock himself in the bathroom. He told the manager he was waiting for her to come back. The state took him in as a ward. He got into fights and was diagnosed with adjustment disorder. He remained a ward of the state until age of eighteen.

Inciting Event:

Malcolm was frequently left by himself. His mother was not available to him, so he created Timmy. Timmy did not speak but was not afraid to take care of himself. To deal with the abuse, she put him through, an alternate identity was formed. He never received treatment for his psychosis. He would have lost time where he had no memory of what he did. He had frequent headaches. No pain medication could get rid of the pain.

Murders:

May 10, 1998, six residents of the Lakeworth Apartments were found stabbed to death. Malcolm was arrested for the murders. He was sentenced to death. The defense had a doctor assess him. Malcolm displayed ten additional identities. It was believed one of his identities was evil and had murdered the six residents.

Psychological aspect:

Malcolm lived in a dysfunctional environment with years of abuse, neglect, watching his mother being arrested. Going with strange men and not knowing who his father was, caused him to formulate other identities.

Among those identities he remained a disturbed nine-year-old boy. A prostitute (mother figure), a police detective (someone he saw arrest his mother), three criminals (probably mother's pimp and clients), a young married couple (possible manager from motel). He formed identities from what he was surrounded by.

It is not clear what triggered the murders. The fact that he committed the crime on his birthday could signify it being a stressor. Could he have committed other murders or crimes each year on his birthday? His blackouts would erase any memory of the crimes.

His identities had names like states. Such as Ed Dakota. Could these be places where he murdered others?

Could Malcolm Rivers have been helped?

Malcolm needed therapy as a child. He was diagnosed with adjustment disorder but received no treatment. The psychologist used behavioral therapy which allowed him to purge his identities. His goal was to have him purge all his identities so he would be left with himself. He did purge all identities but one, Timmy the nine-year-old who happened to be the murderer. He took over as his basic identity. Malcolm was just another identity in the background. He could not be saved once he became an adult.

"The impure are the untouched! The unburned! The unslain! Those who have not been torn have no value in themselves, and no place in this world! They are asleep!" ~ The Beast explaining his own motives.

Split/Glass

Kevin Wendell Crumb

Born unknown Died unknown

Background:

Kevin Wendell Crumb displayed twenty-four distinct personalities. Including one named the Beast. His DID began in childhood due to the abuse by his mother. She showed signs of psychological instability, beating Kevin when things were out of order or unclean. Kevin manifested Dennis an identity suffering from OCD. Patricia was a version of his mother. Hedgwich was a 9-year-old version of himself in the eyes of his mother. The Beast was an identity there to protect Kevin and all the others. The identities gathering the impure for the Beast were called The Horde which consisted of Patricia, Dennis, and Hedgwich. When called by his name Kevin would come forth with no memories. The Horde was able to take over and unleash the Beast.

Inciting Event:

Kevin under the control of Barry worked for the Philadelphia Zoo. While working two teenage girls grabbed his hands and put them on their breasts. Then ran away. This made Barry uncomfortable, but Dennis enjoyed it.

Dennis had a fetish of watching teenage girls dance naked. He had been in trouble for it and when Patricia had him find girls to feed the beast, he chose one to strip and dance for him.

Murders:

The Beast crushed Dr. Fletcher their psychiatrist with his bare hands. He then ate two of the three girls brought to him. One he let go once he saw she was abused too. She had a pure heart and shared the scars of abuse. The Beast still needed to feed on the impure. The Horde kidnapped more girls and was eventually caught with the help of David Dunn. Four girls were saved. They were transported to a rehabilitation facility before going to trial.

Psychological aspect:

His father Clarence Wendell Crumb was on his way to get his mother some help. He never returned. The absence of his father and the constant abuse caused him to create a defense mechanism. Kevin's father was looking at a brochure explaining DID before he died. It could be inferred that Kevin's mother suffered from DID and one of her identities abused Kevin. If this is true, Kevin may have inherited the disorder.

Could Kevin Wendell Crumb have been saved?

Kevin could have been saved earlier in life if his father had not been killed in the train crash. His father was attempting to have his mother receive help for her condition. Without this intervention he was left to fend for himself. As an adult, Kevin went to therapy. His therapist worked with Kevin and was able to keep the Horde away. Using Kevin's full name brought him out. The incident with the girls caused more distress which allowed the Horde to take over and the Beast was created.

The rehabilitation facility used hypnosis lights to control the identities. This kept the Beast from emerging. The Psychiatrist allowed Casey, the only survivor to visit Kevin. She was the only one to bring Kevin out just from her touch. He needed the intimate interaction to feel safe. Kevin could have been saved but it would only work if Casey were with him.

Billy Milligan the first person to use the insanity plea for DID. He was diagnosed as having as many as 24 distinct personalities. He was charged with aggravated robbery, rape, and kidnapping. In 1978 he was committed to Central Ohio Psychiatric Hospital. July 4th, in 1986 he escaped. He was caught and put into another Psychiatric Hospital in Ohio. He was released in 1988 after a psychiatrist found he was no longer a danger to society. In 1991 he was released from all State supervision. In 2014 he died of cancer at the age of 59. Billy was the inspiration for Kevin Wendell Crumb.

Thomas Huskey (Zoo Man) was an ex-employee of the Knoxville Zoo. He would pick up prostitutes and bring them to the Zoo after hours.

He was charged with murder. His confession came from his identity Kyle. Police found four women in different stages of decomposition on Thomas' property. Along with jewelry of the missing women. He had also been charged with rape and under the rape charges he had not used the insanity plea. A jury could not come to a unanimous decision on the murders. Some believed his Kyle identity committed the murders and others believed he was guilty. He was found guilty of rape and was sentenced to 64 years in prison.

Juanita Maxwell had seven personalities. She claimed her persona Wanda had an argument with a 72-year-old woman and she killed her. The woman was found severely beaten, bitten, and choked to death.

Her plea was not guilty by reason of insanity. The judge was convinced she was not aware of what she had done. She was sent to a Psychiatric hospital. She was released in 1988.

Section III

Personality Disorders

According to the American Psychiatric Association, personality is each individual person's way of thinking, feeling, and behaving. We all have a unique personality based on our experiences, upbringing, and inherited traits. Normally, our personality stays consistent.

When someone has a personality disorder, their way of thinking, behavior, and feelings deviates from the societal norms.

Personality disorders consist of borderline personality disorder, antisocial personality disorder, schizotypal personality disorder, paranoid personality disorder, schizoid personality disorder, histrionic personality disorder, narcissistic personality disorder, avoidant personality disorder, dependent personality disorder, and obsessive-compulsive personality disorder.

The villains in this section display extreme deviant personalities.

"I should've killed myself when he put it in me. After the first time, before we were married, Ralph promised never again. He promised and I believed him, but sin never dies... sin never dies, at first it was all right, we lived sinlessly. We slept in the same bed, but we never did it. And then, that night, I saw him looking down at me that way. We got down on our knees to pray for strength. I smelled the whiskey on his breath. Then he took me. He took me, with the filthy roadhouse whiskey on his breath, and I liked it. I liked it, with all that dirty touching of his hands all over me. I should've given you to God when you were Born, but I was weak and backsliding, and now the devil has come home. We'll pray. -Margaret White

Carrie

Margaret White

Born unknown Died Prom night 1980

Background:

Margaret White was deeply religious. She believed anything worldly was sinful. After her father was killed, she opened a fundamentalist church group. There she met Ralph White also deeply religious. They both felt having sexual intercourse even as a married couple was sinful. While dating they had premarital sex and Margaret found out she was pregnant. They were married March 23, 1962.

April 3rd Margaret fell down the stairs and miscarried. Ralph apologized and promised to never have sex again. Sometime in December of 1963, Ralph pressured Margaret for sex after he had been drinking. Margaret hated the act but enjoyed it at the same time. Margaret found out she was pregnant again, but this time carried the baby to term. Ralph left before Carrie was born for another woman.

Throughout Carrie's childhood, Margaret would punish her for any transgression she believed to be sinful. Carrie would be sent to a small closet where she would be required to pray for forgiveness.

Inciting Event:

Carrie started her period during gym. Her gym teacher called Margaret to let her know since Carrie was disturbed and upset. Margaret told Carrie that now she was sinful, and the Devil caused her to bleed. She would have boys touching her now. When Carrie questioned why she was not told, Margaret hit her with one of her bibles and made her go in the closet.

When Carrie was asked to go to Prom, Margaret forbade her.

Carrie was tired of her mother controlling her and stated she was going no matter what she says. Margaret began hurting herself by pulling out her hair, scratching her face, and punching herself.

Carrie left for the Prom. When she returned Margaret pretended to hug her and console her. Then stabbed Carrie in her stomach and pushed her down the stairs. In self-defense Carrie used her telekinesis to throw knives at Margaret killing her.

Psychological aspect:

Margaret showed signs of Scrupulosity a form of Obsessive- Compulsive Personality Disorder. Scrupulosity also known as Religious OCD includes behaviors such as compulsively praying, asking others if you are behaving correctly or analyzing your behavior throughout the day to be sure you are acting appropriately.

It also includes reading or studying religious writings, books, and texts excessively, questioning your motives in numerous situations, excessively apologizing to a deity (God, Allah, etc.) and seeking forgiveness for your behavior.

Could Margaret White have been helped?

Margaret had deep issues regarding her faith. It seems after her father died; she manifested a fanatical religious belief. The treatment for religious OCD is the same used for any of the obsessive-compulsive disorders which includes cognitive behavior therapy, and, in some cases, medication combined with exposure and response therapy. Margaret could still practice her religion but would have been provided alternate ways to handle the triggers.

"Sins? What sins? I am a scientist - I cannot sin."-Dr. Victor Frankenstein

Frankenstein Unbound

Dr. Victor Frankenstein

Born unknown Died unknown

Background:

Dr. Victor Frankenstein was a well-respected scientist in Geneva Switzerland. His experiments were groundbreaking. He wanted to prove man did not need God to create life. He believed science was factual and could be proven. He was wealthy and lived comfortably. His fiancé' was from a prestigious family and he had a six-year-old brother named William. His attempts to create life failed.

In 1817, he figured out a way to bring a man back to life. Using electricity, he could re-animate the body giving life. His creation was larger than the average man, he had superhuman strength, was hard to kill and was naïve.' The creation was aggressive, lonely, easily irritated, and had a murderous rage. Dr. Frankenstein felt he created an abomination and tried to get rid of him.

Inciting Event:

William Frankenstein was killed by the Monster. To keep his experiment a secret, he allowed a young woman to be charged with the death and labeled a witch. The Monster (which some called a beast), killed livestock, caused damage to property, and threatened Dr. Frankenstein to keep killing until he made him a mate.

Psychological Aspect:

Dr. Frankenstein was narcissistic with antisocial behavior. He lied to protect himself and the monster he created. He allowed an innocent young woman to be charged with a murder she did not commit. She was hung and he showed no remorse. When the monster killed his fiancé' he showed no sadness or grief. Instead, he marveled at the fact his monster was better than us in every way. He saw humans as weak and bragged he had made a superior creature.

He took her dead body and lied to the monster about creating his mate. He wanted to revive his dead fiancé. He was successful.

When the monster tried to claim his bride, Dr. Frankenstein called her to him. He let the monster believe he made her for him. The fiancé' afraid of the monster and of what she had become, took Dr. Frankenstein's gun, and shot herself. The monster was infuriated. He grabbed Dr. Frankenstein and broke his spine in half.

Could Dr. Victor Frankenstein have been saved?

Dr. Frankenstein believed strongly in science and felt he was right. He believed we did not have souls. He considered himself like God. He did not take responsibility for the lives his monster took or allowing an innocent young woman to be hung. The only way to help someone who is narcissistic and antisocial is for the person to want to change. Dr. Frankenstein did not.

"Come to Daddy" -Frank Cotton

Hellraiser

Frank Cotton

Born unknown Died unknown

Background:

Frank Cotton was abusive, manipulative, irresponsible and thrill seeking. He did not maintain employment and moved from place to place. He had a gambling problem and was known to disappear for long stretches of time.

He had been arrested several times. His brother Larry always bailed him out. Frank never accepted responsibility for any wrongdoing. He blamed everyone else for his downfall even right before his death.

Inciting Event:

While in Morocco, Frank sought out the Lament configuration which he heard provided intense pleasure. Upon returning home he started to solve the puzzle and opened a gateway to allow the Cenobites into our world. His body was torn apart leaving no trace of him. With the help of his sister-in-law Julia, he was brought back.

Murders:

Frank manipulated Julia to bring men to help him get his body back. Once he was close to being done, he killed his brother for his skin. He also killed Julia.

Psychological aspect:

Frank displayed antisocial personality disorder. According to his brother Larry, he was always a troublemaker, never concerned about consequences. Frank had no conscience, he seduced Julia and had sex with her before their wedding, attempted to rape his niece and kill her. He constantly lied and showed no remorse.

Could Frank Cotton have been helped?

Frank had issues early in life. There had to be some issue with his parents to allow his behavior to continue. Frank needed structure and discipline to learn self-control. Once he became an adult there was no help for him.

"It wanted souls and I brought you!"-Julia Cotton

Julia Cotton

Born unknown Died unknown

Background:

Julia Cotton was married to Larry Cotton. Julia was seduced by Frank, Larry's brother before their wedding. She continued the affair even after they were married. When Frank wanted to leave her, she promised to do anything he wanted to continue the affair.

Inciting Event:

Julia and Larry moved into his childhood home. They were not aware that Frank had been there. Larry cut his hand and went into the attic where Julia was. The blood from his hand revived Frank.

Julia discovered Frank had been killed by the Cenobites.

Remembering her promise to him, Julia agreed to help him come back completely and escape the Cenobites.

Murders:

Julia went out each day looking for men to take home for Frank. She would approach them and offer to do anything they wanted. She led them to the attic and bludgeoned them with a hammer. Sometimes she delivered a fatal blow, sometimes they were just injured. Frank would take them and finish them off. With each kill he got stronger and closer to being alive.

Psychological aspect:

Julia was prone to attention seeking, and mood changes. She always wanted Larry's attention even though she was cheating on him with his brother. She showed signs of having histrionic personality disorder.

Could Julia Cotton have been helped?

Julia was unhappy with Larry but needed the financial stability he offered. If it was not Frank, it may have been someone else who showed her affection. ·To treat her disorder Julia would have needed cognitive therapy. Histrionic personality disorder is difficult to treat, people with this disorder do not see any issue with their behaviors and like to exaggerate. Treatment can be difficult, but some do get help. She would have benefited from group therapy which would have given her outlet to discuss her issues.

"May they burn in hell. Forever and ever in hell."-The Robeson's

The People Under the Stairs.

The Robeson's

Born unknown Died unknown

Background:

The Robeson's come from an extensive line of brother/sister incest. Each generation more insane than the next. They are religious fanatics who used the bible to abuse and punish their children. In their home the children were made to follow a strict speak no evil, hear no evil, and see no evil rule. They wanted the perfect son. But the boys they had always disappointed them. They did not follow the rules. Each rule not followed; father would cut off the offended body part. An ear, an eye, or their tongue. The boys were then put in the cellar. The only one who followed the rules was Alice.

One of the boys got out of the basement and called for help. Father caught him and cut out his tongue. Alice called him Roach and he lived in the walls. Father was adamant about killing him.

No one knew their names. The children only knew them as mother and father. Mother was the authoritarian, making father punish Alice or the children in the basement. She treated him like a child, and he obeyed her.

They were extremely wealthy and initially their family made money selling cheap coffins at extraordinarily marked up prices. Once they got into real estate their profits increased. They bought properties in the ghetto due the cheap prices. They marked up the rent so the tenants would move out and then the buildings demolished for high end condominiums.

The apartments were dilapidated, full of drugs, gang members, and crime. Graffiti on the walls, stray dogs fighting for food, drug addicts sleeping in the hallways.

Inciting Event:

The Robeson's increased the rent and began evictions on the families that could not pay. A young boy nicknamed Fool and his family were the only tenants left in the apartment building. The Robeson's wanted them out so they could build their new high-rise apartments. Fool was coerced into breaking into the Robeson's house to save his sick mother. Once there he discovered Alice and the other children locked in a basement.

Once the Robeson's found out they attempted to kill Fool but failed. He escaped and brought back help.

The Robeson's had been kidnapping children for decades. If they did not obey the children were placed in the basement, starving with no sunlight. Some of the children became cannibalistic. Others died. They had difficulty seeing due to constant living in the dark. They were pale and malnourished. With Fool's help, the boys in the cellar were released. Alice and the children killed the Robeson's.

Murders:

The total number of those killed by The Robeson's is unknown. There were rumors of children disappearing for decades. LeRoy was shot by father and LeRoy's partner was put in the basement and the children ate him.

Psychological aspect:

The Robeson's had generations of deviance and psychological issues running through their veins. Father would complain of headaches when something angered him and beating Alice was the only thing that would stop the pain. When he killed LeRoy, he took him into the basement, strung him up, then cut pieces from him and ate them raw. Then he fed the rest to the children. He liked to wear a black leather bondage suit, it covered him from head to toe.

Mother was very rigid and controlling. They were both paranoid the children would escape so their home was fortified and full of booby traps.

They both had antisocial personality disorder. Mother was also a psychopath. She could go from hysterical to calm and friendly in a matter of minutes. She was abusive and made Alice bathe in scalding hot water. Their issues were genetic.

Could The Robeson's have been helped?

Sometimes there is no way to rehabilitate someone. When the deep- rooted issues are deeply embedded, change is difficult, The Robeson's had generations of deviance.

May 6, 2013, three women were found. They had been chained in a basement. One woman, Amanda Berry was able to scream for help. The neighbor heard her and helped her escape. They had been missing for ten years. Kidnapped and raped, Amanda had a six-year-old daughter. The others had multiple miscarriages. Three brothers were arrested, Ariel, Onil, and Pedro Castro.

Charles Manson was the leader of the cult the Family. He was doomed from the start - Born to a criminal mother and sent around to various family members. He spent more than half his life in detention centers by 1967. Once released he began recruiting followers. He preached of the coming apocalypse and instructed them to kill certain groups of people. In 1969 Susan Atkins, Linda Kasabian, Patricia Krenwinkel, and Tex Watson murdered a pregnant Sharon Tate and four others. The next day they murdered two more. The Family and Charles Manson were given the death penalty but in 1972 California abolished it. Instead, they were sentenced to life without parole.

Andrea Yates murdered her five children by drowning them in the tub. She was convinced the devil was in her home after her son was born in 1994. She murdered her children to keep them from hell. She states she saw the mark of the beast on them. She was sentenced to life in prison. The death penalty was rejected by the court.

Julia Lovemore murdered her six-week-old daughter Faith by stuffing pages of the bible in her mouth then sitting on her until she suffocated her to death. The husband David Lovemore was found shouting and praying after his wife killed their daughter. Julia was held under the Mental Health Act.

Section IV
Paraphilic Disorders

A class of sexual disorders relates to sexual practices and interest. In some cases, sexual interest is so unusual that it is known as a paraphilia— a sexual deviation where sexual arousal is obtained from a consistent pattern of inappropriate responses to objects or people, and in which the behaviors associated with the feelings are distressing and dysfunctional.

Paraphilia's may sometimes be only fantasies, and in other cases may result in actual sexual behavior. The essential feature of a paraphilic disorder, then, is that people with one of these disorders are so psychologically dependent on the target of their desire that they are unable to experience sexual arousal unless the target is present in some form.

♪1, 2, Freddy's coming for you. ♪ ♪3, 4, better lock your door. ♪ ♪5, 6, grab your crucifix. ♪ ♪7, 8, better stay up late. ♪ ♪9, 10, never sleep again. ♪♪

A Nightmare on Elm Street

Freddy Krueger

Born September 1942 Died unknown

Background:

Frederick Charles Krueger (Freddy) Born in Springwood, Ohio to Amanda Krueger. Amanda at the age of eighteen, became a nun. She worked for Westin Hills Hospital taking care of the inmates. On the premises the hospital housed the most deranged and violent offenders in a tower. Amanda was accidentally locked in the tower over the Christmas holiday.

During the three days trapped in the tower, she was beaten and raped by the inmates. She was found bloodied, bruised, and barely alive. When Freddy was born, he was taken by the state as a ward. Mr. Underwood, an alcoholic and abuser, adopted Freddy.

As a young boy he would do disturbing things such as killing small animals. The children would tease him calling him the son of one hundred maniacs. His adopted father abused him and neglected him. Freddy would cut himself and get into trouble as a teenager. Mr. Underwood attempted to beat him with a belt, Freddy tired of the abuse, killed Mr. Underwood.

Freddy as an adult appeared normal. He became a husband and had a daughter. His daughter was the only one that Freddy cared for. He obtained a job through the Power plant working in the boiler room. His urges still plagued him, and he began to kidnap the children of the kids who made fun of him. He mutilated the children and sexually assaulted them.

Inciting Event:

Freddy Krueger's wife discovered a room in the basement where Freddy had pictures of children, several gloves with razors or knives for fingers. The parents of the missing children suspected Freddy as the Springwood Slasher. He was arrested for the rape and murders of children in Springwood. His daughter was taken and put into the foster care system when he was arrested. Her file was sealed so Freddy could not find her.

Due to improper arresting procedure, Freddy was not charged.

When he found out his daughter was taken, he became angry. He decided to kill all the children since they took his. Before he could continue his murder spree, the parents tracked him down to the boiler room where he worked, poured gasoline on the building, and threw Molotov cocktails setting the place on fire, and killing Freddy Krueger.

Murders:

Freddy murdered his wife. He murdered twenty children in Springwood before getting caught. When he returned as a Dream Demon, he killed another 30+ people in their dreams.

Psychological aspect:

Freddy started out having conduct disorder as a teenager. His torturing of animals and self-mutilation are behaviors associated with conduct disorder. As he got older, he displayed antisocial personality disorder along with pedophilic disorder.

Could Freddy Krueger have been helped?

Freddy needed intervention as a child. Proper adoptive parents would have given him a structured home life. If some of his behavior problems stemmed from genetics, he would have benefited from cognitive behavioral therapy and medication.

"You know what, Matt? It's amazing what you can do...when you don't have to look at yourself in the mirror anymore."- Sebastian Caine

Hollow Man

Sebastian Caine

Born unknown Died unknown

Background:

Sebastian Caine a highly intelligent scientist was hired by the Pentagon to create an invisibility serum. He was known for his brilliance and narcissism. The rest of the team overlooked or tolerated his sexist jokes, sarcastic comments, and his pranks.

The invisibility serum had issues initially. The animals who were used as test subjects, either died from the experiment when trying to return visible or became aggressive. Sebastian wanted to take the experiment further and used himself as the human test subject.

Inciting Event:

The serum worked and made Sebastian invisible. He used his invisibility to spy on his team, play more dangerous pranks, and while one of the women on his team slept, he fondled her breast only stopping when she began to wake up.

Invisibility caused Sebastian difficulty sleeping so he attempted his reversing serum which did not work. The longer he remained invisible and relegated to staying in the lab, his mental state deteriorates. He becomes psychotic.

Tired of being locked away, he leaves the lab. He returns to his apartment and watches his neighbor through her window. He enjoys his voyeurism and decides now that he is invisible, she will not know he is in her home. He enters her apartment and rapes her. He returns to the lab undetected.

Murders:

Sebastian murdered his mentor Dr. Kramer to keep him from telling the Pentagon he was successful in making a human invisible. He wanted to keep the serum for himself. When the team found out Sebastian was dangerous, they tried to control him. He killed four of the team members. Linda and Matt were the only survivors. He also killed one of the dogs who he made invisible by throwing him against the cage.

Psychological aspect:

Sebastian was a narcissistic, intelligent man who liked to spy on his female neighbor as she undressed. He had no regard for others, he told inappropriate jokes, he was violent, deceitful, and a liar. His behavior is seen in someone with antisocial personality disorder and voyeuristic disorder.

Could Sebastian Caine have been helped?

Sebastian had no remorse for anything he done. He found no fault with his actions. To have successful treatment, Sebastian would have to take responsibility for his actions, and be willing to change.

Dr. Stanley Dobrowolski between 1985 and 1994 worked in the Student Health Services for Ontario Western University. During that time, he had filmed nine female students during physical exams. In 2004, he was found guilty of touching and hugging female patients without their permission. He had sexual relations with several of his patients. Before his trial in 2014, child pornography was found on his computer. Some produced by Dr. Dobrowolski. He was sentenced to four years in jail.

Jeffrey Polizzi was accused of approaching at least seventy-four women and girls. He would ask inappropriate questions. The police stated Polizzi had prior convictions for voyeurism. In 2009, he was arrested for taking pictures of women in dressing rooms.

George Thomas had filmed over 3,500 people without their knowledge. Including babies and children. He put recording devices in his bathrooms and bedrooms. He also placed devices in public restrooms in London. This went on from 2009-2015 until his recording device was found in the showers at the company gym. George was sentenced to four years in prison.

On July 23, 2007, Joshua Komisarjevsky and Steven Hayes, broke into the home of Dr. William Petit. They violently beat the doctor and made his wife go the bank to take out money. The bank's cameras recorded her withdrawing a considerable sum of money. Regrettably, the police did not arrive to the Petit's home for seven hours. During that time, they raped and killed the 17-year-old daughter, then poured gasoline and set the house on fire.

When they were arrested, it was discovered they targeted the Petit family, watching, following, and taking pictures of the daughters. Komisarjevsky confessed to breaking into homes and watching couples sleeping, he used night vision googles to watch them undetected.

*Confession of a reformed voyeur in his own words
Warning explicit language
It was very intense, the feelings of lust. I had an extremely motivated drive to react to the evil life within me. It wasn't substance driven; it was an overwhelming sense of lust. There were spirits of molesting and violation within my grasp.

I found that looking and happening upon a sexy body was the epitome of my nights and thoughts. I was under a spell of sorts that had me oblivious to moral values.

A felonious being that had a past of abuse and molestation, theft, and poverty. I don't want to sound statistical, or make any to feel sorry for me, this is my story of lows and highs. To make a vision of my struggles I'll say this; I had a troubled life that was not routed to rehab. I was a silent voice also not wanting to be judged and told I was not the victim, and it will be alright.

I had drunken maternity and absent paternity. I had not masculine siblings, I only knew press-on nails and mascara. Nappy hair pulled and a lightened persona, I was amongst the outcasts.

Dirty nails and toes, uncombed hair, snotty nose. Pants ripped and shirts oversized. Going to school to be further ridiculed for the vagabond I looked like. I was the clown in school. Why let someone clown you when I could be the one to make the jokes.

Fuck the rude ass kids who had parents that did something for them. I stay away from the in crowd by hiding under the stairs, I might glimpse a panty or two, while being hidden by the darkness, I felt closest to.

Not having things made me want to have things. But how was I to obtain such things with nothing? You already know the next part. I started stealing little shit like change from the teacher's desk, lockers, and gym bags at recess. When they were at recess I stayed behind to go back to class and take teachers wallets, just to get caught and sent home on suspension.

I was beat for a week, day, and night. Bloody and bruised laying in my bed. I hated my life. It was eventually about to change for the worst. I would go out at night and see what I could find. I'd get a location and solidify that location as my fav peep spot.

I'd visit this residence with the low window that is always cracked, and sometimes open so I can see a shower scene or an amateur pornographic movie. And always on cue, there she was in all her glory.

As time passed, it got more and more intense as more addresses were collected. I'm not a monster, I'm a man who had too much time on his hands. Then as the time progressed, I'd do more.

Now it was opening unlocked windows and getting close to sleeping beauties. Deep sleep was a dream to me. In those deep nights I'd indulge myself from the exposed flesh of a comfortably sleeping unaware spirit. It turned into lightly touching to tasting their flesh without any movement.

It got worse and worse. The more I did, the braver I got. The thing that turned my heart was being away from my family and losing my children by being away for long moments. Cries and heart wrenching pleas to do better from my mother and siblings. But not before home invasions, loitering, and prowling charges kept me inside to think of the things I've done. Now it still lingers, but the acting upon those urges have long since wavered away.

Section V

Trauma and Stress Disorders

Most of us have been through something traumatic in our lives. A death in the family, moving, starting a new school or employment, a divorce, breakup, a marriage.

Some stress is good, like preparing to graduate or opening a new business. How we manage stress varies. Some people meditate, some hold it in, some take out their frustrations on others.

According to the American Psychiatric Association (APA), approximately 60% of men and 50% of women live through at least one traumatic event in their lives, such as accidents, physical assault, sexual abuse, natural disasters, and war combat.

New for the DSM-5, Trauma and stress disorders include posttraumatic stress disorder (PTSD), acute stress disorder, adjustment disorder, reactive attachment disorder, and disinhibited social engagement disorder.

Each Villain in this section has faced some form of Trauma leading them to commit atrocities.

"Everyone isn't bad, Mama! Everything isn't a sin!" – Carrie

Carrietta N. White (Carrie)
Born September 21, 1963, Died Prom night 1980
Background:
Carrietta White known simply as Carrie, born in Chamberlain, Maine to Ralph and Margaret White. Her father left for another woman. His abandonment fueled Margaret's view that Carrie was cursed.

Carrie was abused by her mother and made to pray for forgiveness. Margaret felt everything was sinful; anything red (which she felt was the devil's color), showers, sleeping with pillows, listening to music, watching television, reading books (besides the bible and schoolbooks). Carrie was not allowed to have any friends. This made her an introvert. She was bullied and made fun of starting in Elementary school.

Carrie's mother had a small closet with religious figures and a bible. It was what she called the prayer closet. Whenever Carrie did something sinful in the eyes of Margaret, Carrie was sent to the closet to pray. She would be in there for hours, sometimes days.

Inciting Event:
Margaret neglected to talk to Carrie about menstruation due to her religious beliefs. So, when Carrie started her menstruation during showering after gym class, she became hysterical. Thinking she was bleeding to death; she panicked and asked the girls for help. She was crying uncontrollably. Instead of helping her, they ridiculed her.

Throwing tampons at her. The gym teacher came out and stopped the girls. She slapped Carrie to calm her down. When Carrie arrived home, she asked her mother why she was never told about starting her period. Margaret got mad and said it was the devil's work. She threw hot tea in Carrie's face and hit her with a Bible. She was sent to the closet to pray.

Right before Prom, Tommy Ross approached and asked her to be his date. At first Carrie declined his invitation, afraid of what her mother would do; afraid she was being set up to be made fun of. Tommy came to her house refusing to leave until she said yes.

Carrie agreed just to get him to leave. The more she thought about it the more she wanted to go. She told her mother about the invitation. Her mother adamantly refused to let her go. Carrie, tired of her mother's abuse and controlling behavior, stood up to her.

Her mother tried to hit her, but Carrie stopped her with her telekinesis. The day of the Prom Carrie came out with the dress she had made (red), make-up, and her hair styled. For the first time in her life Carrie felt pretty. Margaret commented that Carrie's "dirty pillows" were showing, and her dress was sinful. She began to attack Carrie, telling her to take the dress off.

Before leaving, Carrie used her telekinesis to push her mother on the bed and held her there until she left the house.

Initially, the Prom was enjoyable. Carrie had never had so much fun. Voting for the King and Queen ballots were passed out. Carrie and Tommy were nominated. Chris Hargensen, the main tormentor, her boyfriend, and several of her friends set up a vicious prank. They swapped the ballots for ones that voted for Carrie and Tommy. Chris and her boyfriend put two buckets of pig's blood in the rafters.

As Chris and her boyfriend hid under the stage with the rope in hand, Carrie and Tommy went on stage to accept their crowns. Chris pulls the rope, dumping the blood on Carrie and Tommy. Then one of the buckets fell and hit Tommy in the head, possibly killing him.

Murders:

Carrie viewed the crowd of students, teachers, and chaperones laughing at her. Carrie's anger intensified. She closed the gym doors, used the water hose to keep anyone from escaping by spraying them with high pressure water.

She killed two teachers. Mr. Fromm, she electrocuted and as his body caught fire, the flames spread. Carrie left the gym trapping everyone inside to burn. Seventy-three high school students died that night.

Chris and her boyfriend escaped the gym and attempted to run Carrie over. Carrie flipped the car killing them. As she walked home, she caused more death and destruction. Killing a total of 440 people. The event was remembered as The Black Prom.

When Carrie arrived home, she washed the pig's blood off, put on pajamas and prepared for bed. Margaret came to her and hugged her. While she hugged her, she took the knife she was hiding and stabbed Carrie in the stomach.

She pushed her down the stairs and tried to stab her again. Carrie used her power to throw knives at her mother. She was so stressed the house began to collapse on her and her mother. Neither one of them survived.

Psychological and Parapsychological aspect:

Carrie had severe PTSD and avoidant personality disorder from her mother's abuse and the constant bullying of her peers. The Prom created acute stress disorder once the stress level peaked Carrie had a psychotic break.

Carrie's telekinesis may have been inherited from her father's side of the family. Her father had another daughter who displayed telekinesis abilities.

Could Carrie White have been helped?

Carrie needed intervention from her mother. She had no other family members she could live with. No teacher intervened to get her any help. The telekinesis could have been controlled with transpersonal psychology and parapsychology. There are several treatments used for PTSD. Medication, Cognitive-behavior therapy (CBT), Hypnosis, and Exposure therapy. Carrie would not be a suitable candidate for Exposure therapy. Not sure if medications would have worked on her. If her mother was involved, no therapy would have worked.

S. L. YARBROUGH

"We have such sights to show you!"- Pinhead

Elliot Spencer (Pinhead)
Born in England 1887 Died date unknown 1920s
Background:
Elliot Spencer was a Captain in the British Expeditionary Force during World War I. He was an empathetic man who felt compassion for those around him. He was an honorable Captain and held others to his high standards. He was a confident man who had a way with words. He had a strong faith in God.
Inciting Event:
In 1918, Elliot participated in the Battle of Flanders. Seeing the carnage and the inhumanity against each other made him lose his faith in man. He blamed God for the destruction. His faith faltered. He felt guilt for not being able to save his fellow soldiers.
Elliot felt he should not be alive. He suffered from severe PTSD blaming himself for the trauma. He traveled around the country a different man. He searched for anything to bring him pleasure. Trying to find something to ease his emotional scars.
While in British controlled India, he found a Lament Configuration. He was told it contained pleasure unlike anything he had ever felt. He purchased the box and took it back to his room.
He solved the box and was visited by Cenobites. He was taken to Hell and made into Pinhead.
Murders:
Pinhead technically did not commit murders. When someone solved the puzzle, the chain of Hell would come and rip them apart. Pinhead and the other Cenobites came to collect their souls.

Psychological aspect:

PTSD is often found in soldiers returning from war. Witnessing your friend or fellow soldiers dying in a brutal fashion, causes trauma that is unforgettable. Anything can trigger the intense feelings. Elliot went from someone who was caring, virtuous, empathetic, trustworthy, and had faith. To someone with no faith, uncaring, pleasure seeking, lost.

Pinhead had forgotten who he was before. When Kirsty showed him a picture of Elliot, he remembered. He felt compassion again which saved Kirsty but caused his demise.

Could Elliot Spencer have been helped?

Elliot (Pinhead) experienced something traumatic and stressful. After the war, with therapy, he could have learned to deal with the stressors. Cognitive-behavioral therapy or Dialectical behavioral therapy along with an antidepressant could have reduced his PTSD.

"When faced with death, who should live versus who will live are two entirely separate things."- Jigsaw

55

Johnathan "John" Kramer (Jigsaw)

Born unknown Died date unknown

Background:

John Kramer, civil engineer, and entrepreneur. He started a company with his friend to build housing for low-income families. Urban Renewal Group who used the motto "Four Walls Build a Home." He also helped his wife, Jill Tuck, with her work at the Homeward Bound Clinic (a clinic for recovering addicts) whose motto was "Cherish your life."

John was an intelligent man and followed the Chinese horoscope. He loved to create toys. When he found out his wife was pregnant with their first child, he was ecstatic. Their unborn child was going to be a boy Born in the year of the pig. John named him Gideon inspired by his first building. John made a child's bed and wooden ventriloquist puppet for his son.

At a party for Homeward Bound, he met William Easton the manager for Umbrella Health an insurance company. Mr. Easton had a mathematical formula he used to decide who would get insurance.

John was disturbed by his method, citing it unethical to decide who lives and who dies. John believed everyone had a will to live and no one should take that away.

Inciting Event:

John became increasingly concerned for his wife and unborn son's safety. Two of Jill's clients got into an altercation and John stepped in. He convinced one of the clients, Cecil, to put his knife away. After the incidence John tried to get Jill to leave her job.

One evening, John came to pick up Jill. As he waited in the car, he watched Cecil run out of the clinic. John went in and found Jill holding her stomach. He rushed her to the hospital, but Gideon could not be saved.

Even after the loss of their son, Jill still wanted to help the people at the clinic. John, feeling angry, told her she couldn't help them; they can only save themselves.

John withdrew himself from everyone. His wife unable to communicate with him, divorced him. He no longer helped with Urban Renewal Group. He stayed in his workshop, often holding the ventriloquist puppet, and stroking his hair.

A few months later he was diagnosed with terminal cancer. John lost his will to live. He drove his car off a cliff hoping to die. He survived. He then realized he wanted to live. He understood people only cherish life when they are on the verge of death. From that point on, John decided with his final days to make people see the value in life.

Murders:

John began his games with his first subject, Cecil. He manufactured extravagant traps in which you had to decide to live or die. John expected a person to be honest with themselves and their crimes.

John didn't commit any murders physically, but he captured people, put them in traps, and their decision killed them.

John recruited others to help him carry out his mission. His health was declining and wanted his games to continue after his death.

Psychological and Philosophical aspect:

John had many stressors in his life, his wife worked in a risky environment which caused the loss of his unborn son. His wife divorced him, then he finds out he has terminal cancer.

He lost interest in his Housing project and helping less fortunate families. He became distant from his wife and business partner. All of these are symptoms of PTSD. Those with PTSD usually have another mental disorder. John suffered from severe depression and was suicidal. It took facing death head on for him to value life.

John displayed high moral values and expected others to adhere to those values. He chose people who were destroying their lives by using drugs for instance. He punished those who committed crimes against others.

Was John bad?

His goals with the traps were to make the subjects realize life was worth fighting for. He made them see the errors of their ways. He saw value in what he was doing. His disciples on the other hand, had no compassion for the guilty. John's traps and riddles could be conquered. His disciples had traps that could not be solved.

Could John Kramer have been helped?
John was a good man who thought he was helping humanity. After the death of his son and the cancer diagnosis, his depression could have been treated with therapy and antidepressants.

Courtney Lockhart was found guilty of abducting, robbing, and fatally shooting Lauren Burke in 2008. He was dishonorably discharged. His ex-fiancé testified he came back from Iraq paranoid. Every night he would hide in the closet and drink heavily. He pulled a gun out and placed it to his head multiple times.

He showed all the signs of PTSD but did not get any help. His defense team tried to argue that he was not in the right state of mind, due to PTSD when he committed the crime. The judge did not accept the argument and sentenced Courtney Lockhart to death.

Certain careers have substantial amounts of people with PTSD. First responders: Fire Fighters, Police, EMS personnel, security staff, and Park Rangers. Unfortunately, majority of first responders don't seek help. They feel the stigma of having a mental disorder, they have the impression it would make them look weak.

Veterans have high rates of PTSD. Because of this, they are more likely to suffer homelessness, and other psychological disorders.

A study performed by the Death Penalty Information Center shows about 300 veterans on death row. Unfortunately, the number of those with PTSD is unknown.

Inanimate Objects and Creatures

Psychosis sometimes is caused by certain places or things. The following have sinister motives. Some have influenced brutal murders; some have stolen the sanity of anyone who spent time there.

The creatures are dangerous and sometimes unescapable.

Haunted Dwellings

Amityville House

Address: 112 Ocean Avenue Long Island, New York.

On November 13, 1974, six family members were killed by the son. Ronald DeFeo Jr. claimed he heard voices telling him to murder his family. He was given 25 years-to-life. He died in prison at the age of 69. He killed his family at age 23. The murders made the home famous. The Lutz family moved in and wrote a book chronicling their year of horrific incidents in the home. Their story turned out to be a hoax. Still the movies based off the history and the Lutz fabrication, were successful. The home was sold in 2006 for $850,000. The new owners moved the home to another lot.

Hill House

The Haunting of Hill House was based on real-life paranormal investigators. Author Shirley Jackson was inspired to draft her novel after reading about a group of researchers renting a house to investigate the paranormal. Although Hill House is not real, the home that it is designed from is in LaGrange, Georgia.

Overlook Hotel

A secluded hotel in the Rocky Mountains. Two caretakers murdered their families and then killed themselves. The hotel was filled with ghosts, causing psychosis in the two male caretakers. Even though there is no real Overlook Hotel, its design was inspired by The Stanley Hotel in Estes Park, Colorado.

True Stories of Haunted and Abandoned Properties you can visit.

Castle Frankenstein Darmstadt, Germany

This 13th century gothic castle was home to Johann Konrad Dippel, an alchemist. There were rumors he would dig up bodies and take them to his lab and perform experiments. What his end goal was no one knows. Mary Shelley, when she was 17, visited a town near Darmstadt. It is speculated Frankenstein was inspired by Johann Dippel.

Murder Mansion Samut Sakhon, Thailand

In 1970 a Chinese-Thai family purchased this opulent mansion. They were successful business owners. One evening, burglars broke in and murdered the father, mother, and child. Stole valuables and were never apprehended. The home has remained vacant, and all the belongings are still there. It appears to have been frozen in time.

Elda Castle Ossining, New York

Constructed by Lucy Abbott Cate, the architect wife of David Thomas Abercrombie (founder of Abercrombie & Fitch), surrounded by 50 acres of wooded land. In 1931, David died, and Lucy abandoned the property. The castle has set empty for 70 years. Vandals and squatters have taken residence over the years. It was listed by Sotheby's for $3.2 million dollars.

Blair Hall Theatre Sinclair Community College Dayton, Ohio

Previously, the gallows for Montgomery County jail harbors the ghost of those hung there. Students in Blair Hall have reported hearing laughter, footsteps, babies crying, feeling like they are being pulled and pressed, when no one's there. Doors slamming and elevators working on their own. A popular story tells of a security guard, seeing a former security chief, who had died a week earlier, walk down the hall.

Woodland Cemetery Dayton Ohio

Many hauntings have been reported at the cemetery, but the most talked about is the little boy named Johnny Morehouse. In 1860, Johnny fell into the Miami & Erie canal. His dog jumped in to save him. He drowned. After he was buried, his dog came to his grave and would not leave. People claim to see Johnny and his dog playing in the cemetery. You can also hear a dog bark at night. There is also a young woman who likes to approach you and start a conversation. Then she disappears.

3557 Stanford Place Dayton, Ohio

3557 Stanford Place, one of four interconnected Townhome apartments. Each one single level with a basement. There were rumors of devil worshippers living there. Three paintings in glow in the dark paint, covered the walls in the basement. A small room painted red with no light was mysteriously situated in a dark corner.

One evening during a party, the younger children were playing Bloody Mary. Screams came from the bedroom. The door would not open, you could hear one of the children trying to turn the knob. The parents also tried to get the door open. Finally, they got in. All the kids ran out crying hysterically saying they saw Bloody Mary.

Whatever entity was in the apartment would appear in the form of someone's imagination. Apparitions looked like figures from album covers. Snakes, bugs, and reptiles would appear at night crawling under blankets and sheets when the lights were off. The apartments remained empty for years and have since been torn down.

The Car 1977

The car, a 1971 Lincoln Continental Mark III black coupe, with dark tinted windows, went on a murderous rampage in the California desert. Ten people were killed, and the car was thought to be destroyed. It was seen later in the streets of Los Angeles.

Christine

Christine was a 1958 Plymouth Fury Vintage. She embodied a vengeful spirit. She was possessive of her owner, killing anyone who got too close or intending to cause her owner harm. Christine killed 13 people before she was destroyed.

The Mangler

The Mangler, a large old laundry machine. Frequent accidents involving the Mangler had occurred. Employees had fallen in or had body parts cut off. It is believed to be possessed. No one has been able to destroy it.

The Event Horizon

The Event Horizon was created by Dr. William Weir. It was a technical marvel. Having the ability to travel faster than light by opening a black hole. With this ability the ship would be able to open a portal to other universes.

On its first voyage, the ship disappeared. All attempts at contact failed. Seven years later it re-appeared, from another dimension liken to what we call Hell. The whole was crew missing. The ship had also become self-aware. Everyone on the ship was manipulated by it.

Hallucinations of their worst fears caused some to commit suicide. The ship used Dr. Weir to protect it. He was killed by the captain separating the drive from the ship and was drawn into the black hole.

One the most famous Haunted highway's is Route 66. Running from Chicago to the Pacific Ocean, travelers claim to see ghost hitchhikers, as well as ghostly encounters at the hotels along the highway.

Archer Avenue in Chicago is listed among the most haunted road. Hooded figures and phantom hearses have been seen. Disappearing Mary, a girl who was killed in a hit and run, has been seen walking the road. Archer Avenue is positioned between two cemeteries.

Make sure not to stop for the bearded hitchhiker on Route 44 in Rehoboth, Mass. Once you let him in, strange things happen. Car radios play static, and his laugh can be heard long after he is gone.

Maud Hughes Road Screaming Bridge in Middletown, Ohio. There have been at least 36 deaths from suicide and accidents on the bridge.

Witnesses say you can hear screams, see ghosts, hooded figures, and mist.

Old Lakeside Park Dayton, Ohio. There are stories told of cars sliding off the road and crashing into the lake off Lakeside Dr. In the late 1800s-1960, there was an Amusement Park and Coliseum at the location. The total number of deaths are unknown. When the highway was expanded in the area, the lake was supposed to be drained. The neighbors thought there would be a parking lot at the bottom. The lake would not drain. The divers could not go far because the water was ice cold, and no bottom was in sight.

The Possession: Dybbuk Box

Dybbuk box is said to house a demon. The box was owned by a woman survivor of the Holocaust. The box is never to be opened, if you do, you release the evil.

Annabelle

Annabelle was a porcelain doll created by Samuel Mullins for his daughter. When Samuel Mullin's daughter, Annabelle was killed, Samuel and his wife were so grief-stricken they prayed to have her back. Instead, they invited a malevolent spirit to inhabit the doll.

The doll possessed by Malthus, terrorizes the Mullins. Over the years other families have owned her. The Warrens took possession of Annabelle and locked her up in a case made of glass from a decommissioned church.

Oculus: Mirror

The Lasser Glass mirror is ornate with silver glass and a black frame. It can cause hallucinations, make someone forget to eat or drink, can intercept phone calls, and mimic the caller. Plants die if they are in the vicinity, and family pets disappear. The mirror cannot be destroyed. Thirteen people have been killed from the influence of the Mirror.

Lament Configuration Lemarchand's Box

In 18th century France, Philip Lemarchand a toy maker, was commissioned to create a puzzle box for Duc de L'Isle, a wealthy nobleman. Duc de L'Isle, preoccupied by dark magic; kills a woman for her skin with the help of his servant. He uses the box to bring forth a demon named Angelique. The skin was used to give Angelique a human form. Philip attempted to make another box, the Elysium Configuration, to send the demons back to Hell. He was killed by Angelique and his bloodline cursed. There are numerous Lament configurations. Lemarchand's box is the only one that can summon the Cenobite's by opening the dimension to Hell.

Both the Dybbuk box and Annabelle can be found in museums. The movie Possession was based of the book describing the events surrounding the box. Annabelle is based off a case paranormal investigator's, the Warrens had. Except the real Annabelle is Raggedy
Ann style doll and not a porcelain doll.

In 2000, an anonymous seller had a painting for sale on eBay. The painting was by Bill Stoneham titled "The Hands Resist Him." It featured a boy and a nightmarish doll next to him. The previous owners said the figures in the painting would move around and sometimes vanish. Anyone who viewed the painting would feel sick and weak. Those who looked at the eBay posting would feel uneasy, dread, or fear.

The Anguished Man is a painting of what looks like a man screaming. The owner inherited the painting from his grandmother. She kept it in the attic due to the paranormal activity when it was displayed. He was told the painting was evil, and the painter used his own blood mixed with the paint. The painter killed himself after he finished. The owner's family had weird things happen once they took ownership of it. They would hear voices crying and see shadowy figures of a man. The owner refuses to sell the painting and keeps it in his basement.

Creatures and Supernatural Being

Alien: Xenomorph's

Xenomorph's are extremely dangerous. To survive they must find a host to replicate. The type of organism used as the host, merges DNA with the Xenomorph. For instance, Xenomorphs from humans stand upright and walk on two legs. Ones from four-legged species will have the attributes of that species.

Their intelligence can vary since their hosts supplies the intellect. There is a life cycle for the Xenomorph. First an egg, laid by the Queen which hatches to form a Facehugger. The Facehugger looks for a host.

Once it finds the host, it attaches to the face. This process initiates the impregnation of the host. After the embryo has gestated, a Chestburster pushes and chews its way out of the host. The final stage is the Adult. The caste system, Drone or worker, Warriors, Praetorians (Protector of the Queen), and Queen. They have acidic blood and are hard to kill. They can adapt to cold but are vulnerable to fire. The Xenomorph appears to only kill to survive. The egg pods stay dormant until a suitable organism arrives. They protect their Queen, killing those who try to harm her.

Predators

Predators are highly skilled warriors. Their species is called Yautja. For centuries, the Yautja have traveled to Earth to hunt. There are five clans, Jungle Predator Clan, Dark Blade Clan, Super Predator Clan, The Killers, and Elite Clan.

Each clan has a ranking system which includes, young bloods (unskilled), bloodied (those who have at least one kill), retirees (older and honored), elite (receive this honor after acquiring the head of a Xenomorph Queen), clan leader (to receive this title an entire Xenomorph hive is killed), adjudicators (law enforcement), bad bloods (criminals), apprentice (honorable humans taken by predators and trained), and ancient (veterans nearly 1000 years old).

The Predators have a strict code most abide by. The Bad Bloods, refuse to abide by the code. They hunt the strongest in a species.

Predators respect any human that is a worthy opponent. They will not attack anyone unarmed or a child. After a kill, they take their trophy from the victim. A spine and skull are normal taken.

Predators have a planet used for hunting. The Bad Bloods hide there. Human criminals are brought there. Xenomorphs are bred by the Yautja, believed to be the ultimate prey are brought there for young bloods to hone their skills. Predators are an intelligent species with advanced weaponry and a code of honor.

Death (Final Destination)

Death has been around since the beginning of time, keeping things in order. As humans we have a set life cycle. Birth, child, teen, adult, elderly, and death. Each stage of our life is automatic. We can't change our date of birth. We can't speed up our life cycle or slow it down. In Final Destination, Alex Browning found a loophole. He was able to trick Death and prolong the inevitable. Death was viewed as a villain, but was he? You could say Death was only doing his job.

Frankenstein's Monster

The monster was lonely. He couldn't interact with the rest of the village. He wasn't intelligent and was naïve' in how the world worked.

He thought all living creatures were created by Dr. Frankenstein. He did not know his strength and killed Dr. Frankenstein's little brother. When asked why he killed him, the monster said he was easy to break, and Dr. Frankenstein should have made him stronger. High pitch noises bothered him. When he heard a police officer blowing a whistle, he became angry and ripped out his heart. He wanted a mate and threatened to keep killing people if Dr.

Frankenstein didn't make him one soon. Dr. Frankenstein didn't care if kept killing, but when his fiancé' was threatened agreed.

He was aggressive and easily aggravated. He killed Dr. Frankenstein because felt betrayed. He promised him a mate but made her for himself. The monster only wanted companionship. If Dr. Frankenstein would have created a mate and explained to the monster how the world worked, he would not have killed anyone.

Section VII

Survivor Instincts

Surviving under insurmountable odds takes an inventive mind, a strong will to survive, and sometimes strong negotiation skills. All the following survivors managed to stay alive with their initial encounters, some only delayed their inevitable death.

"This is Ripley, last survivor of the Nostromo, signing off."

Ellen Ripley

Born January 7, 2092, Death date unknown

Background:

Ellen Ripley was a warrant officer with Weyland-Yutani's commercial freight operations, she was assigned to the USCSS Nostromo in 2122. Ripley and her crew encountered a single Xenomorph. Her crew did not survive. Ripley made it back to Earth and was promoted to Lieutenant First Class but due to her PTSD she lost her position and became a civilian advisor for the Colonial Marines. She was the only person to encounter a Xenomorph and kill it.

With the Colonial Marines, she encountered many more and survived. On one of the expeditions, she rescues a young girl named Newt. She protects her from a Xenomorph Queen. Feeling safe Ripley and the others go into hyper sleep unaware a Xenomorph was onboard. The ship crash landed on Fiorina 161.

Unfortunately, Ripley was the only survivor again. Ripley feels sick and in pain. She figures it is from the crash. The doctor performed a scan and finds she is carrying a Queen embryo. To save humanity, Ripley commits suicide and takes the Queen embryo with her.

What made Ellen Ripley a survivor instead of a victim?

Ellen Ripley when faced with death, chose to fight instead of freeze. Ripley stayed aware of her surroundings having dealt with the xenomorph before she knew how to handle them. Even though she had PTSD and anxiety after being on the Nostromo, she went back out to face her fears. Her sense of self-preservation kept her alive.

"They're not hunting us. We're in the middle of a war."

Alexa "Lex" Woods
Background:
Alexa Woods was an environmental technician who took part in a Weyland Industries expedition to Bouvetøya, Antarctica in 2004 to investigate an ancient Pyramid buried beneath the ice there. She was the top in her field having extensive experience with frozen terrains.

She was hired to be the guide for the team of scientists, archeologists, and technicians. Weyland wanted to reach the pyramid before anyone else did. Alexa refused to take the inexperienced team to an area that was thousands of miles away from civilization, in treacherous temperature and environment. She needed more time to train them. Weyland allowed her to leave and brought in another guide. When Alexa found out who would take her place, she felt uneasy since she knew him, and he was inexperienced in the type of landmass they were heading to.

She decided to stay as their guide. She gave everyone rules to follow, to keep the team safe. When they arrived, a tunnel had already been drilled down to the pyramid. The excavation team set up camp near the tunnel. A cabling system was placed, and they proceeded down the tunnel.

Once they made it to the pyramid, a sacrificial chamber was discovered. When they entered the pyramid, the Xenomorph Queen was hoisted up and started thawing. When she was unfrozen, she began to lay eggs.

Three Predators arrived ready for to hunt the Xenomorphs. The humans were tricked into coming. They needed human hosts for the Xenomorphs. Alexa and Sebastian, the archaeologist, were the only two left.

The others were hosts for the Xenomorphs or were killed by a Predator. Alexa realized they were in the middle of a war between the two species. She had one of the Predator's weapons and planned to give it back. Hoping it would accept it as peace offering. Two of the three Predators were killed by a Xenomorph. Alexa found the remaining Predator and offered him the weapon. He was going to kill her, but a Xenomorph attacked them. Alexa used the Predators weapon and killed the Xenomorph.

The Predator respected her, and they destroyed the pyramid and fought the Xenomorph Queen. Afterwards, the Predator gave her a mark signifying her Xenomorph kill. The Predator was fatally injured by the Queen before her death. The clan members arrived and retrieved their injured clan member. The elderly Predator gave Alexa a weapon to show their appreciation.

What made Alexa "Lex" Woods a survivor instead of a victim?

Alexa trained with her father in situations that took stamina and fearlessness. She worked hard and was serious about her profession. She survived against the Xenomorph by facing her fear and attacking. She showed the Predator she was a worthy ally and gained their respect.

"Happy Halloween, Michael."-Laurie

Laurie Stroud

Born 1961

Background:

Laurie Stroud was born as Cynthia Myers. She was only two years old when her older brother Michael Myers killed their older sister. Michael was committed to the Smith's Grove Sanitarium. She visited him once.

January 3, 1965, her parents die in a car crash. Cynthia is put into the foster care system. Morgan and Pamela Strode adopts her and changes her name to Laurie Strode. The adoption records are sealed so she would be safe from Michael.

Laurie had forgotten about her past and her brother. She was smart and shy. Morgan Strode owned a real estate company Strode Realty. He was hired to sell the Myers home. He had Laurie deliver keys to the home. Michael sees her and begins killing those around her.

What made Laurie Stroud a survivor instead of a victim?

Laurie fought Michael with anything she could make into a weapon. She used a knitting needle, a wire hanger, a butcher knife, and shot him in his eyes. She also ran and hid. Even though she was afraid, she still fought for her survival.

"JASON! ...You've done your job well and mommy is pleased."-Ginny manipulating Jason

Alice Hardy, Ginny Field, Tommy Jarvis
Background:

Alice Hardy was a camp counselor for Camp Crystal Lake. She was hired to help renovate the campgrounds. Alice was dating the son of the former owners the Christy's.

Jason's mother came back once she found out the camp was being reopened. She murdered the counselors, but Alice fought back. Alice wasn't like the rest, she didn't drink, wasn't distracted by having sex, she didn't use drugs. She was alert and fought for survival. She beheaded Mrs. Voorhees and was put into a mental hospital temporarily due to the trauma. Alice was killed by Jason in revenge for his mother.

Ginny Field and her boyfriend Paul had a lodge near Camp Crystal Lake to train camp counselors. Some of the trainees trespassed on Camp Crystal Lake property. Alerting Jason to their location.

He murders the other counselor trainees, Ginny, and Paul escape. In the woods, Ginny comes to a cabin. In the cabin Pamela Voorhees severed head is sitting next to a shrine constructed for her. Her blue sweater is lying next to the head and surrounded by dead bodies.

Ginny knocks Jason out, then she puts on Pamela's sweater and pretends to be her. Jason was fooled at first, bowing in front of Ginny, when he notices his mother's head, he gets up and attacks her.

Paul comes up and wrestles with Jason. While he is distracted Ginny hits him with the machete. They get away. The next day Ginny wakes up while she is being loaded into an ambulance where she is transported to a mental hospital.

Tommy Jarvis, a young teenage boy who loved to make his own prosthetics. He made masks and make up effects. He was the only person to face Jason more than once and survive.

His first encounter with Jason, was at the age of 12. He protects himself and his sister by shaving his head and making himself up to look like a young Jason.

This made Jason confused and distracted long enough for Tommy's sister to strike him with his machete. Jason was not fazed by her. So, Tommy got angry and stabbed Jason repeatedly. This stopped him and allowed them to escape.

Tommy is scarred mentally and is taken to a mental facility. At the age of 18, he escaped one of the many hospitals he was in. He was determined to destroy Jason's body to get rid of the nightmares.

Inadvertently, Tommy revives Jason instead. To get rid of Jason, he would have to be trapped under water where he drowned as a child. Tommy managed to chain him under the water. Tommy was rescued by the sheriff's daughter Megan.

What made Alice, Ginny, and Tommy survivors instead of victims?

Each one had a desire to live. Ginny and Tommy used manipulation to distract Jason and then strike.

"There are No Accidents. No Coincidences. No Escapes. YOU CAN"T CHEAT DEATH."-Bludworth

Alex Browning and Claire Rivers
Background:
Alex Browning was a senior at Mt. Abraham High School. On his way to France for the senior trip, he has a premonition that the plane will crash. He became hysterical and caused himself and six others to be ejected from the plane. They all watch in horror as flight 180 explodes.

Each one of the survivors began to die. At first, their deaths are ruled accidental or suicide. Alex realized they died in the order they were seated on the plane. By saving one, the pattern of death changed. Death missed Alex and Claire.

Claire was Alex's classmate. She helped him to cheat Death. They survived and finished their trip to Paris. Believing they had escaped Death; they dropped their guard. Unfortunately, a brief time later, Alex died from a fallen brick. Claire afraid of Death coming for her, locked herself up in Stonybrook Mental Institution.

Claire was approached by the one of the survivors of a deadly car crash on route 23 which killed 18 people. She was convinced to help so she left the Institution. She was killed and completed the flight 180 survivors.

What made Alex Browning and Claire Rivers survivors instead of victims?
Alex's premonition helped save some of the passengers. He figured out Death's pattern and survived. Claire followed Alex's lead. She stayed alive by locking herself in a facility with nothing to harm her. In the end no one could cheat Death for long.

"Fairy tales ... My father didn't believe in fairy tales either ...Some of them come true, Mr. Ronson. Even the bad ones."

Kristy Cotton

Background:

Kirsty Cotton was the daughter of Larry Cotton, stepdaughter to Julia Cotton and niece of Frank Cotton. Her mother died when she was younger. She despised Julia and was skeptical of her.

Kirsty had a nightmare that her father was killed. Out of concern for her father, she spied on Julia and caught her bringing a strange man into the house. Waiting until she goes in, Kirsty sneaks in the back door.

As she makes her way upstairs, she finds her father. Unbeknownst to her, Uncle Frank had killed her father and took his skin. Kirsty had an altercation with Frank previously while he was first coming back from the dead. She took the lament configuration and mistakenly brought the Cenobites. She negotiated with Pinhead for Frank's soul.

Once she figures out Frank had killed her father, she brought him to the Cenobites. Kirsty reversed the pattern when solving the puzzle box and sent the Cenobites back to Hell.

Kirsty suffered a nervous breakdown and was sent to Channard Institute. Dr. Channard collected puzzle boxes and needed Kirsty and another girl Tiffany to open the doorway. Kirsty came face to face with Pinhead a second time. This time she almost lost her soul, she found an old picture of Pinhead and made him remember he used to be a man.

Kirsty and Tiffany survived. Kirsty found herself facing Pinhead for a third time, she made another deal with Pinhead to bring him souls. She fulfilled her bargain but still lost her soul and became a Cenobite.

What made Kirsty Cotton a survivor instead of a victim?

Kirsty bargained to keep her soul. She is the only one to face Pinhead and survive.

"Your father's one sick mother, you know that? Actually, your mother's one sick mother, too!"-Fool talking to Alice

Poindexter 'Fool' Williams

Background:

Poindexter "Fool" Williams was a young boy whose family lived in a rundown apartment complex. His father was not around, his mother was dying and needed medical treatment. His older sister had young children of her own, she worked but barely made enough for the family.

LeRoy (his sister's boyfriend) had a scheme to rob the landlord's the Robeson's. He convinced Fool to help him and his partner break into the home.

Leroy had Fool dress up like a boy scout and check the home for any security, access into the home, and to check if they were home.

Mother Robeson answered the door and refused to buy anything from him. He needed to get in the house to see what type of security they had. He told Mother Robeson he had to use the bathroom, she refused to allow him in her home.

LeRoy's partner a white man dressed up as a representative of the gas company. He told her he needed access to the basement because of a gas leak in the area. She let him in, but he never came back out.

Fool saw them leave and him and LeRoy went inside to find his partner. The Robeson's came back while Fool and LeRoy was still in the house. Mr. Robeson shot LeRoy and Fool was captured and put in the basement with the cannibal children. Roach, one of the children, gave Fool a bag of gold coins and helped him escape.

Fool catches up the rent, pays for his mother to have medical treatment, and alerts the police about the missing children. He goes back to rescue Alice with the help of others from the apartment complex. They release the children, and they kill the Robeson's. The children had been abducted, missing for years. And now were free.

What made Poindexter "Fool" Williams a survivor instead of a victim?

Fool's need to save his mother overrode his fear of the Robeson's. His anger motivated him to defend himself. Roach helped him survive by protecting him from the others. He was concerned for the other children, and despite the danger to him he went back. He embodied the true spirit of a hero.

"The Beast listened to me. He didn't do what he wanted. You can tell him what to do."-Casey talking to Kevin

Casey Cooke
Background:
Casey Cooke was a high school student kidnapped by the Horde. She was abused by her uncle who gained custody after her father's death. She was an introvert, and her classmates thought she was strange.

When Casey was a little girl, her father took her hunting. Her father showed her how to be patient, quiet, attentive. How to assess her surroundings. She also knew how to use rifle.

All those skills helped her to survive. She remained on high alert due to the sexual abuse she endured from her uncle. Casey told one of the girls to urinate on herself so Dennis wouldn't try to rape her.

She tried to stop the other two girls from fighting their way out. Casey knew you needed to study your opponent first and learn any weakness.

Because of her scars, the beast let her go. She felt a connection with Kevin and all his other personalities. Casey was the only person to bring Kevin to the light by just her touch.

What made Casey Cooke a survivor instead of a victim?

Casey used her survival skills her father taught her. Something she had to use daily. She internalized her pain, hiding her scars from her classmates, teachers, and other adults. Her insight helped her survive.

"Whatever you do, don't fall asleep."-Nancy Thompson

Nancy Thompson, Alice Johnson, Maggie, Tracy, Doc
Background:
Nancy Thompson was one of the children whose parents took part in burning Freddy Krueger. When he came back as a dream demon, he attacked her friends. Killing them one at a time. The police, one of them Nancy's father, investigated the death's calling them suicide.

Nancy's parents did not believe her when she tells them Freddy is the killer. Her mother confesses to helping kill him and shows Nancy Freddy's glove.

The murders continued, and Nancy figured out she could pull Freddy out of her dreams. Once she had him, she could kill him. Her plan worked and Freddy was sent back to hell.

Years later Nancy got a job as an intern for Westin Hills Asylum. Some of the patients began dreaming about Freddy. Then the murders started again. She requests the patients be given Hypnocil so they can sleep without dreaming. The drug was the only reason Nancy was not terrorized by Freddy.

Nancy had to enter the dream realm to save two of the patients she befriended. She saved them but Freddy tricked her and stabbed her with his glove.

Alice Johnson has a unique attribute where she can control her dreams and pull others into her dreams. She was shy, not confident, and unable to defend herself. But in her dreams, she could do or be anything she wanted.

Each time one of her friends died she gained their dream powers.

She was able to use her dream powers to defeat Freddy. Freddy comes back. This time he can manipulate Alice while she is awake. She still has her powers so he can't take her down easy. Alice finds out she is pregnant. Freddy finds out about the baby and hides inside Alice.

Alice tries to release Amanda, Freddy's mother from the dream realm. With help from the other dream warriors, Freddy is defeated. Alice is the only one to defeat Freddy multiple times. She leaves Springwood and the nightmares end.

Freddy had a daughter whose was taken into foster care and adopted. Her name was changed, and the memories of her father were suppressed. Her recurring dreams of a water tower and a little girl plagued her.

The daughter was named Maggie by her adoptive parents. They made sure she never heard anything about Freddy. She worked for a shelter. Freddy found a conduit, the last surviving child from Springwood. Through him he found his daughter.

He killed every child and teenager in Springwood. He wanted more children. By bringing his daughter to Springwood he could use her to leave.

Maggie's co-worker Doc was a psychologist and used dream therapy to help the teenagers there. Tracy was the only one who utilized the dream therapy properly. With the three of them, Maggie brought Freddy out of the dream world. With him in the real world he was defeated and this time it seemed for good.

What made all the above survivors instead of victims?

Nancy found a way to bring Freddy out to set him on fire. Then used a drug to keep him away. She managed to save two victims and lost her life.

Alice had special abilities which made her a worthy adversary against Freddy. She was able to live in peace with her son.

Maggie, Tracy, and Doc used teamwork. They made the dream realm work for them.

"If it bleeds, we can kill it."-Dutch

85

"If it bleeds, we can kill it."-Dutch

Major Alan Schaefer "Dutch"
Born April 1948
Background:
Major Alan "Dutch" Schaefer was head of a special elite military force. After serving in the Army, he was tired of war and fighting. His team went on rescue missions, rejecting any mercenary missions.

His team was hired to rescue a presidential cabinet member from guerrillas in Central America. His team was accompanied by his old friend, George Dillion who now worked for the CIA. They arrived by helicopter and dropped off in the middle of the jungle. Dutch took command and they started their search. They found a helicopter crash. In the trees were the Army Special Soldiers, hanging with their skin removed.

Dutch was on high alert, trying to figure out what type of rebels they were up against. They found the camp heavily guarded. Dutch watched as a captive was assassinated. The team came up with a plan to rescue any remaining prisoners. The team was quick, and the camp destroyed. A woman was found hiding named Anna, Dillion took her as a prisoner. When no presidential member was found, Dillion confessed to lying about the mission. He knew Dutch would not come if it wasn't a rescue mission.

Feeling betrayed and angry, Dutch had to find a way for them to get out of the jungle. As they head for the extraction point, the Predator hunts them. He kills one of the men while he is with Anna but sparing Anna's life. She tells them the creature can blend into the environment.

More of them are killed until it is only Dutch, and Anna left. He tells her to make it to the extraction point and tell them what happened. Dutch figured the Predator did not kill Anna, because she was unarmed.

Dutch runs trying to escape from the Predator, he jumps into a waterfall. The predator jumps in after him. When Dutch reached a shoreline, he had to climb in mud. He hides under branches blending in with the mud. The Predator could not see him.

Dutch realized what he needed to do. He covered himself in mud, made weapons, and set traps. After the traps were set, he yelled out in a warrior like call.

The Predator was skillful and avoided Dutch's trap. The Predator removed his armor, weapons, and helmet challenging Dutch to hand-to-hand combat. Dutch was no match for him. He had one trap left, he released the large counterweight onto the Predator. While he is trapped Dutch asked what he was. The Predator asked Dutch what he was. Then laughed as he set the self-destruct timer. Dutch barely made it. He was picked by the extraction team and made it out safely.

What made Dutch a survivor instead of a victim?

Dutch listened to Anna when she told them what they were up against. He reassessed their tactics and modified them. He accidentally found out how to hide himself from the Predator. His skills in hunting, combat, and intelligence impressed the Predator, he showed Dutch respect when he challenged him. Dutch was an honorable soldier and leader.

"You are one ugly motherfu-"-Lt. Harrigan

Lieutenant Mike Harrigan
Background:

Lieutenant Mike Harrigan was a hot head, insubordinate, and aggressive detective. He had been on the force for 18 years. He was diagnosed with violent behavior, obsessive-compulsive personality disorder, history of excessive force, and aggression level higher than the average officer. The only reason he was still employed was his ten commendations for valor and the best felony arrest record in the department.

Lt. Harrigan was up against gang members, Columbian drug lords, and Jamaican drug lords. His loyalty was to his team, and he did whatever it took to keep them safe.

During one of the hottest summers, the violence from the drug wars brought the Predator to Los Angeles. Gang members and drug lords were killed, skinned, and had their spine and skull removed. Lt. Harrigan searches for a new drug lord.

The DEA comes in and takes over the investigation. Lt. Harrigan doesn't play by the rules and continues his investigation, regrettably causing the death of his best friend and fellow officer.

The government team who took over the investigation was not DEA. They were aware of the Predators, Peter Keyes the head of the government agency debriefed Dutch when he came back from the jungle. Dutch and Anna told them what happened. They assembled a team and waited for contact from the Predator. With the information from Dutch, they set up surveillance tracking the Predator.

Lt. Harrigan followed the Predator to a meat processing plant. The Predator went there every few days to eat. Peter Keyes team set up a trap and made suits to block their heat signature. The Predator had upgraded his helmet so he could see in more than infrared. Keyes team was ambushed. Lt. Harrigan went in to help them.

He puts on a bullet proof vest with a metal plate inserted to protect him from the Predators laser weapon. When he gets into the building, the sprinkler system had been activated. The water from the sprinklers malfunctioned the Predator's suit so he could not camouflage himself.

Lt. Harrigan fights and injures the Predator. He chases him to the roof. He knocks the Predator off the roof, but he grabs Lt. Harrigan and begins the self-destruct sequence. Lt. Harrigan takes the Predator's sphere and cuts his wrist off stopping the self-destruct. The Predator falls and makes his way to his ship. Lt. Harrigan follows him.

They fight again and Lt. Harrigan uses the sphere to cut him from his abdomen to his chest killing the Predator. The Predator's clan arrives to take him back to their planet. The clan leader gives Lt. Harrigan a gun from 1715 and told him to take it.

What made Lieutenant Mike Harrigan a survivor instead of a victim?

Lt. Harrigan's aggressive demeanor and never give up attitude allowed him to severely injure and kill a Predator. He was given a trophy in honor of his kill.

"We're being hunted. The cages. The soldier. All of us."-Royce to Isabelle

Royce and Isabelle

Background:

Royce, Isabelle, and six others found themselves falling with a parachute on. They had been drugged and abandoned on an alien planet. The group consisted of soldiers, mercenaries, criminals, and assassin.

Royce was not a follower and preferred working alone. Since he was a skilled strategist, the others chose to follow his lead. Tracking them were three bad blood Predators. They were larger and ruthless.

They did not abide by the honor code the other clans did. Every year species from all over the galaxy were dropped in for the hunt. The bad bloods hunt the smaller Predators. The hunting parties come in threes.

The bad bloods used tactics from the soldiers in the group. Royce figured out what tactics the Predators used and stayed one step ahead of them. Isabelle was the only one with prior knowledge of Predators. She heard about Dutch and Anna's story; she had never met one but knew one of their weaknesses. She explained how Dutch covered himself in mud so the Predator couldn't see him. The Predators killed two of the group. The Yakuza challenged the Predator in hand-to-hand combat using a sword. The Predator accepted; the Yakuza killed the Predator but lost his life as well. The group found the Predators camp. A smaller Predator was captured and tied to a pole.

Royce used the rest of the group as bait to see the Predators. All three showed up and closed in on them. Isabelle was a sniper; she killed a Predator allowing them to escape.

Noland, the only human survivor on the planet finds them and offers to take them to safety. He has been on the planet for ten seasons. He survived by killing the three Predators who brought his group. He lived in the ship left by the Predators he killed. He stole their armor and uses it to camouflage. The Predators have not been able to find him. He suffered from psychosis talking to a person who wasn't there due to the years of being alone and stress of having to stay hidden.

He tries to set the part of the ship Royce and Isabelle was in on fire. The Predators see the smoke and kill Noland.

Royce and Isabelle work together to defeat the Predator. Royce decides to release the smaller Predator for his help off the planet. The last bad blood and the smaller Predator fight. The bad blood kills the smaller one. Royce attacks him and injures him. Isabelle saves Royce by shooting the Predator.

As they leave the camp, more crates and parachutes come. Royce and Isabelle were determined to find a way off the planet.

What made Royce and Isabelle survivors instead of victims?

Royce changed up tactics to combat the Predators. He fought back and didn't give up. Isabelle's sniper skills saved them. The fact they worked together helped them to defeat the Predator.

"But I will be with you forever, I am ubound."-The monster speaking to Buchanan

Dr. Buchanan

Background:

2031 New Los Angeles, Dr. Buchanan invented a particle beam weapon. He wanted to create a weapon that wouldn't destroy the world. The particle beam would send the enemy through a portal. Dr. Buchanan instead created time loops whenever an item was imploded.

He didn't know how to stop them. A time loop portal opened by his home. He was pulled in and arrived in the countryside in 1817 Geneva. He found a small-town pub. There he met Dr. Frankenstein.

He was enthralled by him. He was curious to see his creation. Dr. Frankenstein denied doing any groundbreaking experiments.

Dr. Buchanan hopped on Dr. Frankenstein's carriage to see for himself. Dr. Frankenstein stopped outside the town and entered the woods. Dr. Buchanan saw him arguing with a monstrous looking man. He was impressed that he created a living being.

Dr. Buchanan followed Dr. Frankenstein and his fiancé 'into a murder trial. A young woman was accused of killing Dr. Frankenstein's little brother. There were witnesses that a beast was killing the livestock. The magistrate did not believe them. It was argued the young woman didn't have the strength to break William Frankenstein's neck. The magistrate accused her of witchcraft and sentenced her to be hung the next day.

Dr. Buchanan recognized the soon to be Mary Shelley. He thought she knew about Frankenstein's monster and could help the young woman. Mary Shelley had no knowledge of the monster. She had only started her book and not sure the direction she was going with it. Dr. Buchanan tried to save the woman. Dr. Frankenstein said he would write a letter telling of her innocence if Dr. Buchanan helped him create a mate for his monster. Dr. Buchanan agreed. He had Dr. Buchanan deliver the letter to his fiancé stating her family had status and could make the magistrate reverse his conviction.

Dr. Frankenstein lied and wrote the letter telling his fiancé to leave town. The woman was hung the next day as scheduled. Dr. Buchanan tried to stop the hanging but was stopped by the crowd.

Dr. Buchanan agreed to help him make a mate after the monster killed his fiancé. He had a plan to open another portal and take all four of them to another timeline. He wanted to stop Dr. Frankenstein and his monster. The timeline they appeared in was like Antarctica. The monster killed Dr. Frankenstein. Dr. Buchanan searched for the monster intent on killing him. He found him in a futuristic power plant.

He shot the monster several times, but he would not die. The power plant had laser beams and controlled by Dr. Buchanan. He used the laser beams to kill the monster.

What made Dr. Buchanan a survivor instead of a victim?

Dr. Buchanan was an honest man and wanted to do what was right. He knew how your creation can become a monster. He wasn't afraid to confront the monster.

What makes someone a villain? Many of our characters were from broken homes, abusive parent or parents, severe stress, or trauma. Others harbored deviant thoughts. Some inherited their disorder. Each one had a stressful event trigger their murderous rage. Carrie and Jason bullied for being different. Elliot (Pinhead), and John (Jigsaw) had major trauma and became the enforcers of morality. Jigsaw giving people the chance to atone for their sins and appreciate life, Pinhead the collector of damned souls.

Michael Myers, Freddy, Sebastian Caine, and The Robeson's were just purely evil. Freddy's father was one of the 100 maniacs who raped his mother. He was conceived through violence, doomed from conception. Michael's motivation for killing was unknown. He seemed to kill for fun. Taking his victims and creatively positioning them as if playing with action figures. Sebastian Caine could see no wrong in his actions. He killed because he could get away with it. The Robeson's were genetically abnormal, cannibalistic, and abusive.

For some, a proper home life would have made the difference.

This is commonly the cause of behavior problems in childhood that turn into psychotic disorders.

What makes someone a survivor? Having a fight instead flight reaction helped most of the survivors. Being aware of the surroundings, using anything as a weapon, studying the opponent for weaknesses, manipulating the situation, and hiding when necessary.

Ellen Ripley, Laurie Stroud, Kirsty Cotton, Tommy Jarvis, and Alice Johnson all encountered their villain more than once and survived. Even though they had PTSD from the previous encounter, they still fought. Laurie and Ellen hid when it was necessary.

Some survivors used strategies, learned about their adversary before fighting back, or teamwork to defeat the villain. Maggie, Tracy, and Doc defeated Freddy, Royce and Isabelle defeated a bad blood Predator, Dutch, and Mike defeated a Predator. Alexa and Mike impressed the Predators and received gifts. There are moments in our lives when we must make choices. Do we submit, fight, accept the inevitable, or hide? We never know until the time comes. I have faced the possibility of death multiple times, as a teenager suffering from a collapsed lung and undergoing major lung surgery twice in the same year. As a young mother, suffering from pre-eclampsia with my twins and an enlarged heart with my son. Four months ago, a stroke which I lost the use of my right hand (dominate side), right leg, speech, and the ability to swallow well. Each time I fought to get better. I chose to fight instead of giving up.

The first time I feared death I was a little girl. I don't want to die anytime soon. I feel I have a lot more to do. I agree with a few of my respondents, my fear now is how I will die, and if there will be suffering. I am thankful for every day and plan to live life to the fullest.

Acknowledgements

I want to take the time to acknowledge my support system and inspiration for the journey.

I would like to thank my beta readers, Tiana Eaton, Nadia Sterling, Tim, and Darion Yarbrough. Your suggestions, editing, and encouraging words helped me to put this all together.

My English Professor, author Tim Waggoner, who told me I could do it and motivated me to finish. My mentor, Dr. Bergdahl, the driving force to help me complete my master's degree. Her support and guidance navigated me through to finish.

The definitions are condensed and focus on the disorders used for the character analysis; they are taken from the DSM-5 manual. For more descriptions and information, I recommend the DSM-5 manual and Understanding Mental Disorders. Your Guide to DSM-5 by the APA.

Schizophrenia spectrum and other psychotic disorders include schizophrenia, other psychotic disorders, and schizotypal (personality) disorder. They are defined by abnormalities in one or more of the following five domains: delusions, hallucinations, disorganized thinking (speech), grossly disorganized or abnormal motor behavior (including catatonia), and negative symptoms.

Key Features That Define the Psychotic Disorders Delusions

Delusions are fixed beliefs that are not amenable to change in light of conflicting evidence. Their content may include a variety of themes (e.g., persecutory, referential, somatic, religious, grandiose).

Persecutory delusions (i.e., belief that one is going to be harmed, harassed, and so forth by an individual, organization, or other group) are most common. Referential delusions (i.e., belief that certain gestures, comments, environmental cues, and so forth are directed at oneself) are also common. Grandiose delusions (i.e., when an individual believes that he or she has exceptional abilities, wealth, or fame) and erotomanic delusions (i.e., when an individual believes falsely that another person is in love with him or her) are also seen. Nihilistic delusions involve the conviction that a major catastrophe will occur, and somatic delusions focus on preoccupations regarding health and organ function.

Delusions are deemed bizarre if they are clearly implausible and not understandable to same-culture peers and do not derive from ordinary life experiences. An example of a bizarre delusion is the belief that an outside force has removed his or her internal organs and replaced them with someone else's organs without leaving any wounds or scars. An example of a nonbizarre delusion is the belief that one is under surveillance by the police, despite a lack of convincing evidence. Delusions that express a loss of control over mind or body are generally considered to be bizarre; these include the belief that one's thoughts have been "removed" by some outside force (thought withdrawal), that alien thoughts have been put into one's mind (thought insertion), or that one's body or actions are being acted on or manipulated by some outside force (delusions of control). The distinction between a delusion and a strongly held idea is sometimes difficult to make and depends in part on the degree of conviction with which the belief is held despite clear or reasonable contradictory evidence regarding its veracity.

Hallucinations

Hallucinations are perception-like experiences that occur without an external stimulus. They are vivid and clear, with the full force and impact of normal perceptions, and not under voluntary control. They may occur in any sensory modality, but auditory hallucinations are the most common in schizophrenia and related disorders. Auditory hallucinations are usually experienced as voices, whether familiar or unfamiliar, that are perceived as distinct from the individual's own thoughts. The hallucinations must occur in the context of a clear sensorium; those that occur while falling asleep (hypnagogic) or waking up (hypnopompic) are considered to be within the range of normal experience. Hallucinations may be a normal part of religious experience in certain cultural contexts.

Disorganized Thinking (Speech)

Disorganized thinking (formal thought disorder) is typically inferred from the individual's speech. The individual may switch from one topic to another (derailment or loose associations). Answers to questions may be obliquely related or completely unrelated (tangentiality). Rarely, speech may be so severely disorganized that it is nearly incomprehensible and resembles receptive aphasia in its linguistic disorganization (incoherence or "word salad"). Because mildly disorganized speech is common and nonspecific, the symptom must be severe enough to substantially impair effective communication. The severity of the impairment may be difficult to evaluate if the person making the diagnosis comes from a different linguistic background than that of the person being examined. Less severe disorganized thinking or speech may occur during the prodromal and residual periods of schizophrenia.

Grossly Disorganized or Abnormal Motor Behavior (including Catatonia)

Grossly disorganized or abnormal motor behavior may manifest itself in a variety of ways, ranging from childlike "silliness" to unpredictable agitation. Problems may be noted in any form of goal-directed behavior, leading to difficulties in performing activities of daily living. Catatonic behavior is a marked decrease in reactivity to the environment. This ranges from resistance to instructions (negativism); to maintaining a rigid, inappropriate or bizarre posture; to a complete lack of verbal and motor responses (mutism and stupor). It can also include purposeless and excessive motor activity without obvious cause (catatonic excitement). Other features are repeated stereotyped movements, staring, grimacing, mutism, and the echoing of speech. Although catatonia has historically been associated with schizophrenia, catatonic symptoms are nonspecific and may occur in other mental disorders (e.g., bipolar or depressive disorders with catatonia) and in medical conditions (catatonic disorder due to another medical condition).

Negative Symptoms

Negative symptoms account for a substantial portion of the morbidity associated with schizophrenia but are less prominent in other psychotic disorders. Two negative symptoms are particularly prominent in schizophrenia: diminished emotional expression and avolition.

Diminished emotional expression includes reductions in the expression of emotions in the face, eye contact, intonation of speech (prosody), and movements of the hand, head, and face that normally give an emotional emphasis to speech. Avolition is a decrease in motivated self-initiated purposeful activities. The individual may sit for long periods of time and show little interest in participating in work or social activities. Other negative symptoms include alogia, anhedonia, and asociality. Alogia is manifested by diminished speech output. Anhedonia is the decreased ability to experience pleasure from positive stimuli or a degradation in the recollection of pleasure previously experienced. Asociality refers to the apparent lack of interest in social interactions and may be associated with avolition, but it can also be a manifestation of limited opportunities for social interactions.

Disorders in This Section

This section is organized along a gradient of psychopathology. Clinicians should first consider conditions that do not reach full criteria for a psychotic disorder or are limited to one domain of psychopathology. Then they should consider time-limited conditions. Finally, the diagnosis of a schizophrenia spectrum disorder requires the exclusion of another condition that may give rise to psychosis.

Schizotypal personality disorder is noted within this chapter as it is considered within the schizophrenia spectrum, although its full description is found in the chapter "Personality Disorders." The diagnosis schizotypal personality disorder captures a pervasive pattern of social and interpersonal deficits, including reduced capacity for close relationships; cognitive or perceptual distortions; and eccentricities of behavior, usually beginning by early adulthood but in some cases first becoming apparent in childhood and adolescence. Abnormalities of beliefs, thinking, and perception are below the threshold for the diagnosis of a psychotic disorder.

Two conditions are defined by abnormalities limited to one domain of psychosis: delusions or catatonia. Delusional disorder is characterized by at least 1 month of delusions but no other psychotic symptoms.

Brief psychotic disorder lasts more than 1 day and remits by 1 month. Schizophreniform disorder is characterized by a symptomatic presentation equivalent to that of schizophrenia except for its duration (less than 6 months) and the absence of a requirement for a decline in functioning.

Schizophrenia lasts for at least 6 months and includes at least 1 month of active-phase symptoms. In schizoaffective disorder, a mood episode and the active-phase symptoms of schizophrenia occur together and were preceded or are followed by at least 2 weeks of delusions or hallucinations without prominent mood symptoms.

Psychotic disorders may be induced by another condition. In substance/medication- induced psychotic disorder, the psychotic symptoms are judged to be a physiological consequence of a drug of abuse, a medication, or toxin exposure and cease after removal of the agent. In psychotic disorder due to another medical condition, the psychotic symptoms are judged to be a direct physiological consequence of another medical condition.

Catatonia can occur in several disorders, including neurodevelopmental, psychotic, bipolar, depressive, and other mental disorders.

Schizophrenia
Diagnostic Criteria 295.90 (F20.9)

- Two (or more) of the following, each present for a significant portion of time during a 1 -month period (or less if successfully treated). At least one of these must be (1), (2), or (3):
- Delusions. 2. Hallucinations. 3. Disorganized speech (e.g., frequent derailment or incoherence). 4. Grossly disorganized or catatonic behavior. 5. Negative symptoms (i.e., diminished emotional expression or avolition).
- For a significant portion of the time since the onset of the disturbance, level of functioning in one or more major areas, such as work, interpersonal relations, or self-care, is markedly below the level achieved prior to the onset (or when the onset is in childhood or adolescence, there is failure to achieve expected level of interpersonal, academic, or occupational functioning).
- Continuous signs of the disturbance persist for at least 6 months. This 6-month period must include at least 1 month of symptoms (or less if successfully treated) that meet Criterion A (i.e., active-phase symptoms) and may include periods of prodromal or residual symptoms. During these prodromal or residual periods, the signs of the disturbance may be manifested by only negative symptoms or by two or more symptoms listed in Criterion A present in an attenuated form (e.g., odd beliefs, unusual perceptual experiences).
- Schizoaffective disorder and depressive or bipolar disorder with psychotic features have been ruled out because either 1) no major depressive or manic episodes have occurred concurrently with the active-phase symptoms, or 2) if mood episodes have occurred during active-phase symptoms, they have been present for a minority of the total duration of the active and residual periods of the illness.
- The disturbance is not attributable to the physiological effects of a substance (e.g., a drug of abuse, a medication) or another medical condition.
- If there is a history of autism spectrum disorder or a communication disorder of childhood onset, the additional diagnosis of schizophrenia

is made only if prominent delusions or hallucinations, in addition to the other required symptoms of schizophrenia, are also present for at least 1 month (or less if successfully treated).

- Specify if: The following course specifiers are only to be used after a 1year duration of the disorder and if they are not in contradiction to the diagnostic course criteria.

First episode, currently in acute episode: First manifestation of the disorder meeting the defining diagnostic symptom and time criteria.

An acute episode is a time period in which the symptom criteria are fulfilled.

First episode, currently in partial remission: Partial remission is a period of time during which an improvement after a previous episode is maintained and in which the defining criteria of the disorder are only partially fulfilled.

First episode, currently in full remission: Full remission is a period of time after a previous episode during which no disorder-specific symptoms are present.

Multiple episodes, currently in acute episode: Multiple episodes may be determined after a minimum of two episodes (i.e., after a first episode, a remission and a minimum of one relapse).

Multiple episodes, currently in partial remission

Multiple episodes, currently in full remission

Continuous: Symptoms fulfilling the diagnostic symptom criteria of the disorder are remaining for the majority of the illness course, with subthreshold symptom periods being very brief relative to the overall course.

Unspecified

Specify if:

With catatonia (refer to the criteria for catatonia associated with another mental disorder, pp. 119-120, for definition).

Specify current severity:

Severity is rated by a quantitative assessment of the primary symptoms of psychosis, including delusions, hallucinations, disorganized speech, abnormal psychomotor behavior, and negative symptoms. Each of these symptoms may be rated for its current severity (most severe in the last 7 days) on a 5-point scale ranging from 0 (not present) to 4 (present and severe). **Note:** Diagnosis of schizophrenia can be made without using this severity specifier.

Associated Features Supporting Diagnosis

Individuals with schizophrenia may display inappropriate affect (e.g., laughing in the absence of an appropriate stimulus); a dysphoric mood that can take the form of depression, anxiety, or anger; a disturbed sleep pattern (e.g., daytime sleeping and nighttime activity); and a lack of interest in eating or food refusal. Depersonalization, derealization, and somatic concerns may occur and sometimes reach delusional proportions. Anxiety and phobias are common. Cognitive deficits in schizophrenia are common and are strongly linked to vocational and functional impairments. These deficits can include decrements in declarative memory, working memory, language function, and other executive functions, as well as slower processing speed. Abnormalities in sensory processing and inhibitory capacity, as well as reductions in attention, are also found.

Some individuals with schizophrenia show social cognition deficits, including deficits in the ability to infer the intentions of other people (theory of mind), and may attend to and then interpret irrelevant events or stimuli as meaningful, perhaps leading to the generation of explanatory delusions. These impairments frequently persist during symptomatic remission.

Some individuals with psychosis may lack insight or awareness of their disorder (i.e., anosognosia). This lack of "insight" includes unawareness of symptoms of schizophrenia and may be present throughout the entire course of the illness. Unawareness of illness is typically a symptom of schizophrenia itself rather than a coping strategy. It is comparable to the lack of awareness of neurological deficits following brain damage, termed anosognosia. This symptom is the most common predictor of non-adherence to treatment, and it predicts higher relapse rates, increased number of involuntary treatments, poorer psycho-social functioning, aggression, and a poorer course of illness.

Hostility and aggression can be associated with schizophrenia, although spontaneous or random assault is uncommon. Aggression is more frequent for younger males and for individuals with a past history of violence, non-adherence with treatment, substance abuse, and impulsivity. It should be noted that the vast majority of persons with schizophrenia are not aggressive and are more frequently victimized than are individuals in the general population.

Currently, there are no radiological, laboratory, or psychometric tests for the disorder. Differences are evident in multiple brain regions between groups of healthy individuals and persons with schizophrenia, including evidence from neuroimaging, neuropathological, and neurophysiological studies. Differences are also evident in cellular architecture, white matter connectivity, and gray matter volume in a variety of regions such as the pre-frontal and temporal cortices. Reduced overall brain volume has been observed, as well as increased brain volume reduction with age. Brain volume reductions with age are more pronounced in individuals with schizophrenia than in healthy individuals. Finally, individuals with schizophrenia appear to differ from individuals without the disorder in eye- tracking and electrophysiological indices.

Neurological soft signs common in individuals with schizophrenia include impairments in motor coordination, sensory integration, and motor sequencing of complex movements; left-right confusion; and disinhibition of associated movements. In addition, minor physical anomalies of the face and limbs may occur.

Prevalence

The lifetime prevalence of schizophrenia appears to be approximately 0.3%-0.7%. Delusions are called bizarre when they are clearly impossible to happen in real life.

Development and Course

The psychotic features of schizophrenia typically emerge between the late teens and the mid-30s; onset prior to adolescence is rare. The peak age at onset for the first psychotic episode is in the early- to mid-20s for males and in the late-20s for females. The onset may be abrupt or insidious, but the majority of individuals manifest a slow and gradual development of a variety of clinically significant signs and symptoms.

Half of these individuals complain of depressive symptoms. Earlier age at onset has traditionally been seen as a predictor of worse prognosis.

However, the effect of age at onset is likely related to gender, with males having worse premorbid adjustment, lower educational achievement, more prominent negative symptoms and cognitive impairment, and in general a worse outcome. Impaired cognition is common, and alterations in cognition are present during development and precede the emergence of psychosis, taking the form of stable cognitive impairments during adulthood. Cognitive impairments may persist when other symptoms are in remission and contribute to the disability of the disease.

The predictors of course and outcome are largely unexplained, and course and outcome may not be reliably predicted. The course appears to be favorable in about 20% of those with schizophrenia, and a small number of individuals are reported to recover completely.

However, most individuals with schizophrenia still require formal or informal daily living supports, and many remain chronically ill, with exacerbations and remissions of active symptoms, while others have a course of progressive deterioration.

Psychotic symptoms tend to diminish over the life course, perhaps in association with normal age-related declines in dopamine activity. Negative symptoms are more closely related to prognosis than are positive symptoms and tend to be the most persistent.

Furthermore, cognitive deficits associated with the illness may not improve over the course of the illness.

The essential features of schizophrenia are the same in childhood, but it is more difficult to make the diagnosis. In children, delusions and hallucinations may be less elaborate than in adults, and visual hallucinations are more common and should be distinguished from normal fantasy play. Disorganized speech occurs in many disorders with childhood onset (e.g., autism spectrum disorder), as does disorganized behavior (e.g., attention-deficit/hyperactivity disorder). These symptoms should not be attributed to schizophrenia without due consideration of the more common disorders of childhood. Childhood-onset cases tend to resemble poor-outcome adult cases, with gradual onset and prominent negative symptoms. Children who later receive the diagnosis of schizophrenia are more likely to have experienced nonspecific emotional-behavioral disturbances and psychopathology, intellectual and language alterations, and subtle motor delays.

Late-onset cases (i.e., onset after age 40 years) are overrepresented by females, who may have married. Often, the course is characterized by a predominance of psychotic symptoms with preservation of affect and social functioning. Such late-onset cases can still meet the diagnostic criteria for schizophrenia, but it is not yet clear whether this is the same condition as schizophrenia diagnosed prior to mid-life (e.g., prior to age 55 years).

Differential Diagnosis

Major depressive or bipolar disorder with psychotic or catatonic features. The distinction between schizophrenia and major depressive or bipolar disorder with psychotic features or with catatonia depends on the temporal relationship between the mood disturbance and the psychosis, and on the severity of the depressive or manic symptoms. If delusions or hallucinations occur exclusively during a major depressive or manic episode, the diagnosis is depressive or bipolar disorder with psychotic features.

Schizoaffective disorder. A diagnosis of schizoaffective disorder requires that a major depressive or manic episode occur concurrently with the active-phase symptoms and that the mood symptoms be present for a majority of the total duration of the active periods.

Schizophreniform disorder and brief psychotic disorder. These disorders are of shorter duration than schizophrenia as specified in Criterion C, which requires 6 months of symptoms. In schizophreniform disorder, the disturbance is present less than 6 months, and in brief psychotic disorder, symptoms are present at least 1 day but less than 1 month.

Delusional disorder. Delusional disorder can be distinguished from schizophrenia by the absence of the other symptoms characteristic of schizophrenia (e.g., delusions, prominent auditory or visual hallucinations, disorganized speech, grossly disorganized or catatonic behavior, negative symptoms).

Schizotypal personality disorder. Schizotypal personality disorder may be distinguished from schizophrenia by subthreshold symptoms that are associated with persistent personality features.

Obsessive-compulsive disorder and body dysmorphic disorder. Individuals with obsessive-compulsive disorder and body dysmorphic disorder
may present with poor or absent insight, and the preoccupations may reach delusional proportions. But these disorders are distinguished from schizophrenia by their prominent obsessions, compulsions, preoccupations with appearance or body odor, hoarding, or body-focused repetitive behaviors.

Posttraumatic stress disorder. Posttraumatic stress disorder may include flashbacks that have a hallucinatory quality, and hypervigilance may reach paranoid proportions. But a traumatic event and characteristic symptom features relating to reliving or reacting to the event are required to make the diagnosis.

Autism spectrum disorder or communication disorders. These disorders may also have symptoms resembling a psychotic episode but are distinguished by their respective deficits in social interaction with repetitive and restricted behaviors and other cognitive and communication deficits. An individual with autism spectrum disorder or communication disorder must have symptoms that meet full criteria for schizophrenia, with prominent hallucinations or delusions for at least 1 month, in order to be diagnosed with schizophrenia as a comorbid condition.

Other mental disorders associated with a psychotic episode. The diagnosis of schizophrenia is made only when the psychotic episode is persistent and not attributable to the physiological effects of a substance or another medical condition. Individuals with a delirium or major or minor neurocognitive disorder may present with psychotic symptoms, but these would have a temporal relationship to the onset of cognitive changes consistent with those disorders.

Individuals with substance/medication-induced psychotic disorder may present with symptoms characteristic of Criterion A for schizophrenia, but the substance/medication-induced psychotic disorder can usually be distinguished by the chronological relationship of substance use to the onset and remission of the psychosis in the absence of substance use.

Comorbidity

Rates of comorbidity with substance-related disorders are high in schizophrenia. Over half of individuals with schizophrenia have tobacco use disorder and smoke cigarettes regularly. Comorbidity with anxiety disorders is increasingly recognized in schizophrenia. Rates of obsessive-compulsive disorder and panic disorder are elevated in individuals with schizophrenia compared with the general population. Schizotypal or paranoid personality disorder may sometimes precede the onset of schizophrenia.

Life expectancy is reduced in individuals with schizophrenia because of associated medical conditions. Weight gain, diabetes, metabolic syndrome, and cardiovascular and pulmonary disease are more common in schizophrenia than in the general population. Poor engagement in health maintenance behaviors (e.g., cancer screening, exercise) increases the risk of chronic disease, but other disorder factors, including medications, lifestyle, cigarette smoking, and diet, may also play a role. A shared vulnerability for psychosis and medical disorders may explain some of the medical comorbidity of schizophrenia.

Treatment

Schizophrenia has no cure. Usually, Antipsychotic drugs are prescribed. Taken daily, the delusions can be reduced or even stop.

Two types of medications are used. First generation or typical are dugs that have been around since mid-1950's. The drugs included are haloperidol, fluphenazine, and perphenazine.

The other type is second generation or atypical and were introduced in the 1990's. These include risperidone, olanzapine, and quetiapine.

Finally, Cognitive Behavioral Therapy (CBT) helps by focusing on the thinking and behavior. CBT helps instruct the person with Schizophrenia to test the reality of their thoughts and perceptions. Medication and CBT are successful when used together.

Dissociative disorders are characterized by a disruption of and/or discontinuity in the normal integration of consciousness, memory, identity, emotion, perception, body representation, motor control, and behavior. Dissociative symptoms can potentially disrupt every area of psychological functioning. This includes dissociative identity disorder, dissociative amnesia, depersonalization/derealization disorder, other specified dissociative disorder, and unspecified dissociative disorder.

Dissociative symptoms are experienced as a) unbidden intrusions into awareness and behavior, with accompanying losses of continuity in subjective experience (i.e., "positive" dissociative symptoms such as fragmentation of identity, depersonalization, and derealization) and/or

b) inability to access information or to control mental functions that normally are readily amenable to access or control (i.e., "negative" dissociative symptoms such as amnesia).

The dissociative disorders are frequently found in the aftermath of trauma, and many of the symptoms, including embarrassment and confusion about the symptoms or a desire to hide them, are influenced by the proximity to trauma. In DSM-5, the dissociative disorders are placed next to, but are not part of, the trauma and stressor-related disorders, reflecting the close relationship between these diagnostic classes. Both acute stress disorder and posttraumatic stress disorder contain dissociative symptoms, such as amnesia, flashbacks, numbing, and depersonalization/derealization.

Depersonalization/derealization disorder is characterized by clinically significant persistent or recurrent depersonalization (i.e., experiences of unreality or detachment from one's mind, self, or body) and/or derealization (i.e., experiences of unreality or detachment from one's surroundings). These alterations of experience are accompanied by intact reality testing. There is no evidence of any distinction between individuals with predominantly depersonalization versus derealization symptoms. Therefore, individuals with this disorder can have depersonalization, derealization, or both.

Dissociative amnesia is characterized by an inability to recall autobiographical information. This amnesia may be localized (i.e., an event or period of time), selective (i.e., a specific aspect of an event), or generalized (i.e., identity and life history). Dissociative amnesia is fundamentally an inability to recall autobiographical information that is inconsistent with normal forgetting. It may or may not involve purposeful travel or bewildered wandering (i.e., fugue). Although some individuals with amnesia promptly notice that they have "lost time" or that they have a gap in their memory, most individuals with dissociative disorders are initially unaware of their amnesias. For them, awareness of amnesia occurs only when personal identity is lost or when circumstances make these individuals aware that autobiographical information is missing (e.g., when they discover evidence of events they cannot recall or when others tell them or ask them about events they cannot recall). Until and unless this happens, these individuals have "amnesia for their amnesia." Amnesia is experienced as an essential feature of dissociative amnesia; individuals may experience localized or selective amnesia most commonly, or generalized amnesia rarely.

Dissociative fugue is rare in persons with dissociative amnesia but common in dissociative identity disorder. Dissociative identity disorder is characterized by a) the presence of two or more distinct personality states or an experience of possession and b) recurrent episodes of amnesia.

The fragmentation of identity may vary with culture (e.g., possession form presentations) and circumstance. Thus, individuals may experience discontinuities in identity and memory that may not be immediately evident to others or are obscured by attempts to hide dysfunction. Individuals with dissociative identity disorder experience:

a) recurrent, inexplicable intrusions into their conscious functioning and sense of self (e.g., voices; dissociated actions and speech; intrusive thoughts, emotions, and impulses), b) alterations of sense of self (e.g., attitudes, preferences, and feeling like one's body or actions are not one's own), c) odd changes of perception (e.g., depersonalization or derealization, such as feeling detached from one's body while cutting), and d) intermittent functional neurological symptoms. Stress often produces transient exacerbation of dissociative symptoms that makes them more evident.

The residual category of other specified dissociative disorder has seven examples: chronic or recurrent mixed dissociative symptoms that approach, but fall short of, the diagnostic criteria for dissociative identity disorder;

dissociative states secondary to brainwashing or thought reform; two acute presentations, of less than 1 month's duration, of mixed dissociative symptoms, one of which is also marked by the presence of psychotic symptoms; and three single-symptom dissociative presentations—dissociative trance, dissociative stupor or coma, and Ganser's syndrome (the giving of approximate and vague answers).

Dissociative Identity Disorder Diagnostic Criteria 300.14 (F44.81)

- Disruption of identity characterized by two or more distinct personality states, which may be described in some cultures as an experience of possession. The disruption in identity involves marked discontinuity in sense of self and sense of agency, accompanied by related alterations in affect, behavior, consciousness, memory, perception, cognition, and/or sensory-motor functioning. These signs and symptoms may be observed by others or reported by the individual.

- Recurrent gaps in the recall of everyday events, important personal information, and/ or traumatic events that are inconsistent with ordinary forgetting.

- The symptoms cause clinically significant distress or impairment in social, occupational, or other important areas of functioning.

- The disturbance is not a normal part of a broadly accepted cultural or religious practice. Note: In children, the symptoms are not better explained by imaginary playmates or other fantasy play.

- The symptoms are not attributable to the physiological effects of a substance (e.g., blackouts or chaotic behavior during alcohol intoxication) or another medical condition (e.g., complex partial seizures).

-

Diagnostic Features

The defining feature of dissociative identity disorder is the presence of two or more distinct personality states or an experience of possession (Criterion A). The overtness or covertness of these personality states, however, varies as a function of psychological motivation, current level of stress, culture, internal conflicts and dynamics, and emotional resilience. Sustained periods of identity disruption may occur when psychosocial pressures are severe and/or prolonged. In many possession-form cases of dissociative identity disorder, and in a small proportion of non-possession-form cases, manifestations of alternate identities are highly overt. Most individuals with non-possession-form dissociative identity disorder do not overtly display their discontinuity of identity for long periods of time, only a small minority present to clinical attention with observable alternation of identities. When alternate personality states are not directly observed, the disorder can be identified by two clusters of symptoms: 1) sudden alterations or discontinuities in sense of self and sense of agency (Criterion A), and

2) recurrent dissociative amnesias (Criterion B).

Criterion A symptoms are related to discontinuities of experience that can affect any aspect of an individual's functioning. Individuals with dissociative identity disorder may report the feeling that they have suddenly become depersonalized observers of their "own" speech and actions, which they may feel powerless to stop (sense of self). Such individuals may also report perceptions of voices (e.g., a child's voice; crying; the voice of a spiritual being). In some cases, voices are experienced as multiple, perplexing, independent thought streams over which the individual experiences no control.

Strong emotions, impulses, and even speech or other actions may suddenly emerge, without a sense of personal ownership or control (sense of agency). These emotions and impulses are frequently reported as ego-dystonic and puzzling. Attitudes, outlooks, and personal preferences (e.g., about food, activities, dress) may suddenly shift and then shift back. Individuals may report that their bodies feel different (e.g., like a small child, like the opposite gender, huge and muscular). Alterations in sense of self and loss of personal agency may be accompanied by a feeling that these attitudes, emotions, and behaviors—even one's body—are "not mine" and/or are "not under my control." Although most Criterion A symptoms are subjective, many of these sudden discontinuities in speech, affect, and behavior can be witnessed by family, friends, or the clinician. Non-epileptic seizures and other conversion symptoms are prominent in some presentations of dissociative identity disorder, especially in some non-Western settings.

The dissociative amnesia of individuals with dissociative identity disorder manifests in three primary ways: as 1) gaps in remote memory of personal life events (e.g., periods of childhood or adolescence; some important life events, such as the death of a grandparent, getting married, giving birth); 2) lapses in dependable memory (e.g., of what happened today, of well-learned skills such as how to do their job, use a computer, read, drive); and 3) discovery of evidence of their everyday actions and tasks that they do not recollect doing (e.g., finding unexplained objects in their shopping bags or among their possessions; finding perplexing writings or drawings that they must have created; discovering injuries; "coming to" in the midst of doing something).

Dissociative fugues, wherein the person discovers dissociated travel, are common. Thus, individuals with dissociative identity disorder may report that they have suddenly found themselves at the beach, at work, in a night- club, or somewhere at home (e.g., in the closet, on a bed or sofa, in the corner) with no memory of how they came to be there. Amnesia in individuals with dissociative identity disorder is not limited to stressful or traumatic events; these individuals often cannot recall everyday events as well.

Individuals with dissociative identity disorder vary in their awareness and attitude toward their amnesias. It is common for these individuals to minimize their amnestic symptoms. Some of their amnestic behaviors may be apparent to others—as when these persons do not recall something they were witnessed to have done or said, when they cannot remember their own name, or when they do not recognize their spouse, children, or close friends.

Possession-form identities in dissociative identity disorder typically manifest as behaviors that appear as if a "spirit," supernatural being, or outside person has taken control, such that the individual begins speaking or acting in a distinctly different manner. For example, an individual's behavior may give the appearance that her identity has been replaced by the "ghost" of a girl who committed suicide in the same community years before, speaking and acting as though she were still alive. Or an individual may be "taken over" by a demon or deity, resulting in profound impairment, and demanding that the individual or a relative be punished for a past act, followed by more subtle periods of identity alteration.

However, the majority of possession states around the world are normal, usually part of spiritual practice, and do not meet criteria for dissociative identity disorder. The identities that arise during possession-form dissociative identity disorder present recurrently, are unwanted and involuntary, cause clinically significant distress or impairment (Criterion C), and are not a normal part of a broadly accepted cultural or religious practice (Criterion D).

Associated Features Supporting Diagnosis

Individuals with dissociative identity disorder typically present with comorbid depression, anxiety, substance abuse, self-injury, nonepileptic seizures, or another common symptom. They often conceal, or are not fully aware of, disruptions in consciousness, amnesia, or other dissociative symptoms. Many individuals with dissociative identity disorder report dissociative flashbacks during which they undergo a sensory reliving of a previous event as though it were occurring in the present, often with a change of identity, a partial or complete loss of contact with or disorientation to current reality during the flashback, and a subsequent amnesia for the content of the flashback. Individuals with the disorder typically report multiple types of interpersonal maltreatment during childhood and adulthood.

Nonmaltreatment forms of overwhelming early life events, such as multiple long, painful, early-life medical procedures, also may be reported. Self-mutilation and suicidal behavior are frequent. On standardized measures, these individuals report higher levels of hypnotizability and dissociativity compared with other clinical groups and healthy control subjects. Some individuals experience transient psychotic phenomena or episodes. Several brain regions have been implicated in the pathophysiology of dissociative identity disorder, including the orbitofrontal cortex, hippocampus, parahippocampal gyrus, and amygdala.

Prevalence

The 12-month prevalence of dissociative identity disorder among adults in a small U.S. community study was 1.5%. The prevalence across genders in that study was 1.6% for males and 1.4% for females.

Development and Course

Dissociative identity disorder is associated with overwhelming experiences, traumatic events, and/or abuse occurring in childhood.

The full disorder may first manifest at almost any age (from earliest childhood to late life). Dissociation in children may generate problems with memory, concentration, attachment, and traumatic play.

Nevertheless, children usually do not present with identity changes; instead, they present primarily with overlap and interference among mental states (Criterion A phenomena), with symptoms related to discontinuities of experience. Sudden changes in identity during adolescence may appear to be just adolescent turmoil or the early stages of another mental disorder. Older individuals may present to treatment with what appear to be late-life mood disorders, obsessive-compulsive disorder, paranoia, psychotic mood disorders, or even cognitive disorders due to dissociative amnesia. In some cases, disruptive affects and memories may increasingly intrude into awareness with advancing age.

Psychological decompensation and overt changes in identity may be triggered by 1) removal from the traumatizing situation (e.g., through leaving home); 2) the individual's children reaching the same age at which the individual was originally abused or traumatized; 3) later traumatic experiences, even seemingly inconsequential ones, like a minor motor vehicle accident; or 4) the death of, or the onset of a fatal illness in, their abuser(s).

Risk and Prognostic Factors

Environmental. Interpersonal physical and sexual abuse is associated with an increased risk of dissociative identity disorder. Prevalence of childhood abuse and neglect in the United States, Canada, and Europe among those with the disorder is about 90%. Other forms of traumatizing experiences, including childhood medical and surgical procedures, war, childhood prostitution, and terrorism, have been reported.

Course modifiers. Ongoing abuse, later-life re-traumatization, comorbidity with mental disorders, severe medical illness, and delay in appropriate treatment are associated with poorer prognosis.

Personality Disorders

This section begins with a general definition of personality disorder that applies to each of the 10 specific personality disorders. A personality disorder is an enduring pattern of inner experience and behavior that deviates markedly from the expectations of the individual's culture, is pervasive and inflexible, has an onset in adolescence or early adult- hood, is stable over time, and leads to distress or impairment.

With any ongoing review process, especially one of this complexity, different viewpoints emerge, and an effort was made to accommodate them. Thus, personality disorders are included in both Sections II and III. The material in Section II represents an update of text associated with the same criteria found in DSM-IV-TR, whereas Section III includes the proposed research model for personality disorder diagnosis and conceptualization developed by the DSM-5 Personality and Personality Disorders Work Group. As this field evolves, it is hoped that both versions will serve clinical practice and research initiatives, respectively.

The following personality disorders are included in this section.

- Paranoid personality disorder is a pattern of distrust and suspiciousness such that others' motives are interpreted as malevolent.

- Schizoid personality disorder is a pattern of detachment from social relationships and a restricted range of emotional expression.

- Schizotypal personality disorder is a pattern of acute discomfort in close relationships, cognitive or perceptual distortions, and eccentricities of behavior.

- Antisocial personality disorder is a pattern of disregard for, and violation of, the rights of others.

- Borderline personality disorder is a pattern of instability in interpersonal relationships, self-image, and affects, and marked impulsivity.

- Histrionic personality disorder is a pattern of excessive emotionality and attention seeking.

- Narcissistic personality disorder is a pattern of grandiosity, need for admiration, and lack of empathy.

- Avoidant personality disorder is a pattern of social inhibition, feelings of inadequacy, and hypersensitivity to negative evaluation.

- Dependent personality disorder is a pattern of submissive and clinging behavior related to an excessive need to be taken care of.

- Obsessive-compulsive personality disorder is a pattern of preoccupation with orderliness, perfectionism, and control.

- Personality change due to another medical condition is a persistent personality disturbance that is judged to be due to the direct physiological effects of a medical condition (e.g., frontal lobe lesion).

- Other specified personality disorder and unspecified personality disorder is a cate- gory provided for two situations: 1) the individual's personality pattern meets the general criteria for a personality disorder, and traits of several different personality disorders are present, but the criteria for any specific personality disorder are not met; or 2) the individual's personality pattern meets the general criteria for a personality disorder, but the individual is considered to have a personality disorder that is not included in the DSM-5 classification (e.g., passive-aggressive personality disorder).

The personality disorders are grouped into three clusters based on descriptive similarities. Cluster A includes paranoid, schizoid, and schizotypal personality disorders. Individuals with these disorders often appear odd or eccentric.

Cluster B includes antisocial, borderline, histrionic, and narcissistic personality disorders. Individuals with these disorders often appear dramatic, emotional, or erratic. Cluster C includes avoidant, dependent, and obsessive- compulsive personality disorders. Individuals with these disorders often appear anxious or fearful. It should be noted that this clustering system, although useful in some research and educational situations, has serious limitations and has not been consistently validated.

Moreover, individuals frequently present with co-occurring personality disorders from different clusters. Prevalence estimates for the different clusters suggest 5.7% for dis- orders in Cluster A, 1.5% for disorders in Cluster B, 6.0% for disorders in Cluster C, and 9.1% for any personality disorder, indicating frequent co-occurrence of disorders from different clusters. Data from the 2001-2002 National Epidemiologic Survey on Alcohol and Related Conditions suggest that approximately 15% of U.S. adults have at least one personality disorder.

Dimensional Models for Personality Disorders

The diagnostic approach used in this manual represents the categorical perspective that personality disorders are qualitatively distinct clinical syndromes. An alternative to the categorical approach is the dimensional perspective that personality disorders represent maladaptive variants of personality traits that merge imperceptibly into normality and into one another. See Section III for a full description of a dimensional model for personality disorders. The DSM-IV personality disorder clusters (i.e., odd-eccentric, dramatic- emotional, and anxious-fearful) may also be viewed as dimensions representing spectra of personality dysfunction on a continuum with other mental disorders. The alternative dimensional models have much in common and together appear to cover the important areas of personality dysfunction. Their integration, clinical utility, and relationship with the personality disorder diagnostic categories and various aspects of personality dysfunction are under active investigation.

Cluster B Personality Disorders Antisocial Personality Disorder Diagnostic Criteria 301.7 (F60.2)

• A pervasive pattern of disregard for and violation of the rights of others, occurring since age 15 years, as indicated by three (or more) of the following:

• Failure to conform to social norms with respect to lawful behaviors, as indicated by repeatedly performing acts that are grounds for arrest.

• Deceitfulness, as indicated by repeated lying, use of aliases, or conning others for personal profit or pleasure.

• Impulsivity or failure to plan ahead.

• Irritability and aggressiveness, as indicated by repeated physical fights or assaults.

1. Reckless disregard for safety of self or others.
2. Consistent irresponsibility, as indicated by repeated failure to sustain consistent work behavior or honor financial obligations.
3. Lack of remorse, as indicated by being indifferent to or rationalizing having hurt, mistreated, or stolen from another.
4. The individual is at least age 18 years.
5. . There is evidence of conduct disorder with onset before age 15 years.
6. The occurrence of antisocial behavior is not exclusively during the course of schizophrenia or bipolar disorder.

Diagnostic Features

The essential feature of antisocial personality disorder is a pervasive pattern of disregard for, and violation of, the rights of others that begins in childhood or early adolescence and continues into adulthood. This pattern has also been referred to as psychopathy, sociopathy, or dyssocial personality disorder. Because deceit and manipulation are central features of antisocial personality disorder, it may be especially helpful to integrate information acquired from systematic clinical assessment with information collected from collateral sources.

For this diagnosis to be given, the individual must be at least age 18 years (Criterion B) and must have had a history of some symptoms of conduct disorder before age 15 years (Criterion C).

Conduct disorder involves a repetitive and persistent pattern of behavior in which the basic rights of others or major age-appropriate societal norms or rules are violated. The specific behaviors characteristic of conduct disorder falls into one of four categories: aggression to people and animals, destruction of property, deceitfulness or theft, or serious violation of rules.

The pattern of antisocial behavior continues into adulthood. Individuals with antisocial personality disorder fail to conform to social norms with respect to lawful behavior (Criterion A1). They may repeatedly perform acts that are grounds for arrest (whether they are arrested or not), such as destroying property, harassing others, stealing, or pursuing illegal occupations. Persons with this disorder disregard the wishes, rights, or feelings of others. They are frequently deceitful and manipulative in order to gain personal profit or pleasure (e.g., to obtain money, sex, or power) (Criterion A2). They may repeatedly lie, use an alias, con others, or malinger. A pattern of impulsivity may be manifested by a failure to plan ahead (Criterion A3). Decisions are made on the spur of the moment, without forethought and without consideration for the consequences to self or others; this may lead to sudden changes of jobs, residences, or relationships.

Individuals with antisocial personality disorder tend to be irritable and aggressive and may repeatedly get into physical fights or commit acts of physical assault (including spouse beating or child beating) (Criterion A4). (Aggressive acts that are required to defend oneself or someone else are not considered to be evidence for this item.) These individuals also display a reckless disregard for the safety of themselves or others (Criterion A5). This may be evidenced in their driving behavior (i.e., recurrent speeding, driving while intoxicated, multiple accidents). They may engage in sexual behavior or substance use that has a high risk for harmful consequences. They may neglect or fail to care for a child in a way that puts the child in danger.

Individuals with antisocial personality disorder also tend to be consistently and extremely irresponsible (Criterion A6). Irresponsible work behavior may be indicated by significant periods of unemployment despite available job opportunities, or by abandonment of several jobs without a realistic plan for getting another job. There may also be a pattern of repeated absences from work that are not explained by illness either in themselves or in their family. Financial irresponsibility is indicated by acts such as defaulting on debts, failing to provide child support, or failing to support other dependents on a regular basis. Individuals with antisocial personality disorder show little remorse for the consequences of their acts (Criterion A7). They may be indifferent to, or provide a superficial rationalization for, having hurt, mistreated, or stolen from someone (e.g., 'Life's unfair," "losers deserve to lose"). These individuals may blame the victims for being foolish, helpless, or deserving their fate (e.g., "he had it coming anyway"); they may minimize the harmful consequences of their actions; or they may simply indicate complete indifference. They generally fail to compensate or make amends for their behavior. They may believe that everyone is out to "help number one" and that one should stop at nothing to avoid being pushed around.

The antisocial behavior must not occur exclusively during the course of schizophrenia or bipolar disorder (Criterion D).

Associated Features Supporting Diagnosis

Individuals with antisocial personality disorder frequently lack empathy and tend to be callous, cynical, and contemptuous of the feelings, rights, and sufferings of others. They may have an inflated and arrogant self-appraisal (e.g., feel that ordinary work is beneath them or lack a realistic concern about their current problems or their future) and may be excessively opinionated, self-assured, or cocky. They may display a glib, superficial charm and can be quite voluble and verbally facile (e.g., using technical terms or jargon that might impress someone who is unfamiliar with the topic). Lack of empathy, inflated self-appraisal, and superficial charm are features that have been commonly included in traditional conceptions of psychopathy that may be particularly distinguishing of the disorder and more predictive of recidivism in prison or forensic settings, where criminal, delinquent, or aggressive acts are likely to be nonspecific. These individuals may also be irresponsible and exploitative in their sexual relationships. They may have a history of many sexual partners and may never have sustained a monogamous relationship. They may be irresponsible as parents, as evidenced by malnutrition of a child, an illness in the child resulting from a lack of minimal hygiene, a child's dependence on neighbors or nonresident relatives for food or shelter, a failure to arrange for a caretaker for a young child when the individual is away from home, or repeated squandering of money required for household necessities. These individuals may receive dishonorable discharges from the armed services, may fail to be self-supporting, may become impoverished or even homeless, or may spend many years in penal institutions.

Individuals with antisocial personality disorder are more likely than people in the general population to die prematurely by violent means (e.g., suicide, accidents, homicides). Individuals with antisocial personality disorder may also experience dysphoria, including complaints of tension, inability to tolerate boredom, and depressed mood. They may have associated anxiety disorders, depressive disorders, substance use disorders, somatic symptom disorder, gambling disorder, and other disorders of impulse control. Individuals with antisocial personality disorder also often have personality features that meet criteria for other personality disorders, particularly borderline, histrionic, and narcissistic personality disorders. The likelihood of developing antisocial personality disorder in adult life is increased if the individual experienced childhood onset of conduct disorder (before age 10 years) and accompanying attention deficit/hyperactivity disorder. Child abuse or neglect, unstable or erratic parenting, or inconsistent parental discipline may increase the likelihood that conduct disorder will evolve into antisocial personality disorder.

Prevalence

Twelve-month prevalence rates of antisocial personality disorder, using criteria from previous DSMs, are between 0.2% and 3.3%. The highest prevalence of antisocial personality disorder (greater than 70%) is among most severe samples of males with alcohol use disorder and from substance abuse clinics, prisons, or other forensic settings.

Prevalence is higher in samples affected by adverse socioeconomic (i.e., poverty) or sociocultural (i.e., migration) factors.

Development and Course

Antisocial personality disorder has a chronic course but may become less evident or remit as the individual grows older, particularly by the fourth decade of life. Although this remission tends to be particularly evident with respect to engaging in criminal behavior, there is likely to be a decrease in the full spectrum of antisocial behaviors and substance use. By definition, antisocial personality cannot be diagnosed before age 18 years.

Risk and Prognostic Factors

Genetic and physiological. Antisocial personality disorder is more common among the first-degree biological relatives of those with the disorder than in the general population. The risk to biological relatives of females with the disorder tends to be higher than the risk to biological relatives of males with the disorder. Biological relatives of individuals with this disorder are also at increased risk for somatic symptom disorder and substance use disorders. Within a family that has a member with antisocial personality disorder, males more often have antisocial personality disorder and substance use disorders, whereas females more often have somatic symptom disorder.

However, in such families, there is an increase in prevalence of all these disorders in both males and females compared with the general population. Adoption studies indicate that both genetic and environmental factors contribute to the risk of developing antisocial personality disorder. Both adopted and biological children of parents with antisocial personality disorder have an increased risk of developing antisocial personality disorder, somatic symptom disorder, and substance abuse disorders. Adopted-away children resemble their biological parents more than their adoptive parents, but the adoptive family environment influences the risk of developing a personality disorder and related psychopathology.

Histrionic Personality Disorder Diagnostic Criteria 301.50 (F60.4)

A pervasive pattern of excessive emotionality and attention seeking, beginning by early adulthood and present in a variety of contexts, as indicated by five (or more) of the following:

1. Is uncomfortable in situations in which he or she is not the center of attention.
2. Interaction with others is often characterized by inappropriate sexually seductive or provocative behavior.
3. Displays rapidly shifting and shallow expression of emotions.
4. Consistently uses physical appearance to draw attention to self.
5. Has a style of speech that is excessively impressionistic and lacking in

detail.

6. Shows self-dramatization, theatricality, and exaggerated expression of emotion.

1. Is suggestible (i.e., easily influenced by others or circumstances).
2. Considers relationships to be more intimate than they actually are.

Diagnostic Features

The essential feature of histrionic personality disorder is pervasive and excessive emotionality and attention-seeking behavior. This pattern begins by early adulthood and is present in a variety of contexts.

Individuals with histrionic personality disorder are uncomfortable or feel unappreciated when they are not the center of attention (Criterion 1). Often lively and dramatic, they tend to draw attention to themselves and may initially charm new acquaintances by their enthusiasm, apparent openness, or flirtatiousness. These qualities wear thin, however, as these individuals continually demand to be the center of attention. They commandeer the role of "the life of the party." If they are not the center of attention, they may do something dramatic (e.g., make up stories, create a scene) to draw the focus of attention to themselves. This need is often apparent in their behavior with a clinician (e.g., being flattering, bringing gifts, providing dramatic descriptions of physical and psychological symptoms that are replaced by new symptoms each visit).

The appearance and behavior of individuals with this disorder are often inappropriately sexually provocative or seductive (Criterion 2). This behavior not only is directed toward persons in whom the individual has a sexual or romantic interest but also occurs in a wide variety of social, occupational, and professional relationships beyond what is appropriate for the social context. Emotional expression may be shallow and rapidly shifting (Criterion 3). Individuals with this disorder consistently use physical appearance to draw attention to themselves (Criterion 4). They are overly concerned with impressing others by their appearance and expend an excessive amount of time, energy, and money on clothes and grooming. They may "fish for compliments" regarding appearance and may be easily and excessively upset by a critical comment about how they look or by a photograph that they regard as unflattering.

These individuals have a style of speech that is excessively impressionistic and lacking in detail (Criterion 5). Strong opinions are expressed with dramatic flair, but underlying reasons are usually vague and diffuse, without supporting facts and details. For example, an individual with histrionic personality disorder may comment that a certain individual is a wonderful human being yet be unable to provide any specific examples of good qualities to support this opinion.

Individuals with this disorder are characterized by self-dramatization, theatricality, and an exaggerated expression of emotion (Criterion 6). They may embarrass friends and acquaintances by an excessive public display of emotions (e.g., embracing casual acquaintances with excessive ardor, sobbing uncontrollably on minor sentimental occasions, having temper tantrums). However, their emotions often seem to be turned on and off too quickly to be deeply felt, which may lead others to accuse the individual of faking these feelings.

Individuals with histrionic personality disorder have a high degree of suggestibility (Criterion 7). Their opinions and feelings are easily influenced by others and by current fads. They may be overly trusting, especially of strong authority figures whom they see as magically solving their problems. They have a tendency to play hunches and to adopt convictions quickly. Individuals with this disorder often consider relationships more intimate than they are, describing almost every acquaintance as "my dear, dear friend" or referring to physicians met only once or twice under professional circumstances by their first names (Criterion 8).

Associated Features Supporting Diagnosis

Individuals with histrionic personality disorder may have difficulty achieving emotional intimacy in romantic or sexual relationships. Without being aware of it, they often act out a role (e.g., "victim" or "princess") in their relationships to others. They may seek to control their partner through emotional manipulation or seductiveness on one level, while displaying a marked dependency on them at another level. Individuals with this disorder often have impaired relationships with same-sex friends because their sexually provocative interpersonal style may seem a threat to their friends' relationships. These individuals may also alienate friends with demands for constant attention. They often become depressed and upset when they are not the center of attention. They may crave novelty, stimulation, and excitement and have a tendency to become bored with their usual routine. These individuals are often intolerant of, or frustrated by, situations that involve delayed gratification, and their actions are often directed at obtaining immediate satisfaction. Although they often initiate a job or project with great enthusiasm, their interest may lag quickly. Longer term relationships may be neglected to make way for the excitement of new relationships.

The actual risk of suicide is not known, but clinical experience suggests that individuals with this disorder are at increased risk for suicidal gestures and threats to get attention and coerce better caregiving. Histrionic personality disorder has been associated with higher rates of somatic symptom disorder, conversion disorder (functional neurological symptom disorder), and major depressive disorder. Borderline, narcissistic, antisocial, and dependent personality disorders often co-occur.

Prevalence

Data from the 2001-2002 National Epidemiologic Survey on Alcohol and Related Conditions suggest a prevalence of histrionic personality of 1.84%.

Differential Diagnosis

Other personality disorders and personality traits. Other personality disorders may be confused with histrionic personality disorder because they have certain features in common. It is therefore important to distinguish among these disorders based on differences in their characteristic features. However, if an individual has personality features that meet criteria for one or more personality disorders in addition to histrionic personality disorder, all can be diagnosed.

Although borderline personality disorder can also be characterized by attention seeking, manipulative behavior, and rapidly shifting emotions, it is distinguished by self-destructiveness, angry disruptions in close relationships, and chronic feelings of deep emptiness and identity disturbance.

Individuals with antisocial personality disorder and histrionic personality disorder share a tendency to be impulsive, superficial, excitement seeking, reckless, seductive, and manipulative, but persons with histrionic personality disorder tend to be more exaggerated in their emotions and do not characteristically engage in antisocial behaviors. Individuals with histrionic personality disorder are manipulative to gain nurturance, whereas those with antisocial personality disorder are manipulative to gain profit, power, or some other material gratification. Although individuals with narcissistic personality disorder also crave attention from others, they usually want praise for their "'superiority," whereas individuals with histrionic personality disorder are willing to be viewed as fragile or dependent if this is instrumental in getting attention. Individuals with narcissistic personality disorder may exaggerate the intimacy of their relationships with other people, but they are more apt to emphasize the "VIP" status or wealth of their friends. In dependent personality disorder, the individual is excessively dependent on others for praise and guidance, but is without the flamboyant, exaggerated, emotional features of individuals with histrionic personality disorder.

Many individuals may display histrionic personality traits. Only when these traits are inflexible, maladaptive, and persisting and cause significant functional impairment or subjective distress do they constitute histrionic personality disorder.

Personality changes due to another medical condition. Histrionic personality disorder must be distinguished from personality change due to another medical condition, in which the traits that emerge are attributable to the effects of another medical condition on the central nervous system. Substance use disorders. The disorder must also be distinguished from symptoms that may develop in association with persistent substance use.

Narcissistic Personality Disorder Diagnostic Criteria 301.81 (F60.81)

A pervasive pattern of grandiosity (in fantasy or behavior), need for admiration, and lack of empathy, beginning by early adulthood and present in a variety of contexts, as indicated by five (or more) of the following:

Has a grandiose sense of self-importance (e.g., exaggerates achievements and talents, expects to be recognized as superior without commensurate achievements).

1. Is preoccupied with fantasies of unlimited success, power, brilliance, beauty, or ideal love.
2. Believes that he or she is "special" and unique and can only be understood by, or should associate with, other special or high-status

   people (or institutions).

3. Requires excessive admiration.
4. Has a sense of entitlement (i.e., unreasonable expectations of especially favorable treatment or automatic compliance with his or her expectations).
5. Is interpersonally exploitative (i.e., takes advantage of others to achieve his or her own ends).
6. Lacks empathy is unwilling to recognize or identify with the feelings and needs of others.
7. Is often envious of others or believes that others are envious of him or her.
8. Shows arrogant, haughty behaviors or attitudes.
9.

Diagnostic Features

The essential feature of narcissistic personality disorder is a pervasive pattern of grandiosity, need for admiration, and lack of empathy that begins by early adulthood and is present in a variety of contexts.

Individuals with this disorder have a grandiose sense of self- importance (Criterion 1). They routinely overestimate their abilities and inflate their accomplishments, often appearing boastful and pretentious. They may blithely assume that others attribute the same value to their efforts and may be surprised when the praise they expect and feel they deserve is not forthcoming. Often implicit in the inflated judgments of their own accomplishments is an underestimation (devaluation) of the contributions of others.

Individuals with narcissistic personality disorder are often preoccupied with fantasies of unlimited success, power, brilliance, beauty, or ideal love (Criterion 2). They may ruminate about "'long overdue" admiration and privilege and compare themselves favorably with famous or privileged people. Individuals with narcissistic personality disorder believe that they are superior, special, or unique and expect others to recognize them as such (Criterion 3). They may feel that they can only be understood by, and should only associate with, other people who are special or of high status and may attribute "unique," "perfect," or "gifted" qualities to those with whom they associate.

Individuals with this disorder believe that their needs are special and beyond the ken of ordinary people. Their own self-esteem is enhanced (i.e., "mirrored") by the idealized value that they assign to those with whom they associate. They are likely to insist on having only the "top" person (doctor, lawyer, hairdresser, instructor) or being affiliated with the "best" institutions but may devalue the credentials of those who disappoint them.

Individuals with this disorder generally require excessive admiration (Criterion 4). Their self-esteem is almost invariably very fragile. They may be preoccupied with how well they are doing and how favorably they are regarded by others. This often takes the form of a need for constant attention and admiration. They may expect their arrival to be greeted with great fanfare and are astonished if others do not covet their possessions. They may constantly fish for compliments, often with great charm. A sense of entitlement is evident in these individuals' unreasonable expectation of especially favorable treatment (Criterion 5). They expect to be catered to and are puzzled or furious when this does not happen. For example, they may assume that they do not have to wait in line and that their priorities are so important that others should defer to them, and then get irritated when others fail to assist "in their very important work." This sense of entitlement, combined with a lack of sensitivity to the wants and needs of others, may result in the conscious or unwitting exploitation of others (Criterion 6). They expect to be given whatever they want or feel they need, no matter what it might mean to others.

For example, these individuals may expect great dedication from others and may overwork them without regard for the impact on their lives. They tend to form friendships or romantic relationships only if the other person seems likely to advance their purposes or otherwise enhance their self-esteem. They often usurp special privileges and extra resources that they believe they deserve because they are so special.

Individuals with narcissistic personality disorder generally have a lack of empathy and have difficulty recognizing the desires, subjective experiences, and feelings of others (Criterion 7). They may assume that others are totally concerned about their welfare. They tend to discuss their own concerns in inappropriate and lengthy detail, while failing to recognize that others also have feelings and needs.

They are often contemptuous and impatient with others who talk about their own problems and concerns.

These individuals may be oblivious to the hurt their remarks may inflict (e.g., exuberantly telling a former lover that "I am now in the relationship of a lifetime!"; boasting of health in front of someone who is sick). When recognized, the needs, desires, or feelings of others are likely to be viewed disparagingly as signs of weakness or vulnerability. Those who relate to individuals with narcissistic personality disorder typically find an emotional coldness and lack of reciprocal interest.

These individuals are often envious of others or believe that others are envious of them (Criterion 8). They may begrudge others their successes or possessions, feeling that they better deserve those achievements, admiration, or privileges. They may harshly devalue the contributions of others, particularly when those individuals have received acknowledgment or praise for their accomplishments. Arrogant, haughty behaviors characterize these individuals; they often display snobbish, disdainful, or patronizing attitudes (Criterion 9). For example, an individual with this disorder may complain about a clumsy waiter's "rudeness" or "stupidity" or conclude a medical evaluation with a condescending evaluation of the physician.

Associated Features Supporting Diagnosis

Vulnerability in self-esteem makes individuals with narcissistic personality disorder very sensitive to "injury" from criticism or defeat.

Although they may not show it outwardly, criticism may haunt these individuals and may leave them feeling humiliated, degraded, hollow, and empty. They may react with disdain, rage, or defiant counterattack. Such experiences often lead to social withdrawal or an appearance of humility that may mask and protect the grandiosity.

Interpersonal relations are typically impaired because of problems derived from entitlement, the need for admiration, and the relative disregard for the sensitivities of others. Though overweening ambition and confidence may lead to high achievement, performance may be disrupted because of intolerance of criticism or defeat. Sometimes vocational functioning can be very low, reflecting an unwillingness to take a risk in competitive or other situations in which defeat is possible. Sustained feelings of shame or humiliation and the attendant self-criticism may be associated with social withdrawal, depressed mood, and persistent depressive disorder (dysthymia) or major depressive disorder. In contrast, sustained periods of grandiosity may be associated with a hypomanic mood. Narcissistic personality disorder is also associated with anorexia nervosa and substance use disorders (especially related to cocaine). Histrionic, borderline, antisocial, and paranoid personality disorders may be associated with narcissistic personality disorder.

Prevalence

Prevalence estimates for narcissistic personality disorder, based on DSM-IV definitions, range from 0% to 6.2% in community samples.

Development and Course

Narcissistic traits may be particularly common in adolescents and do not necessarily indicate that the individual will go on to have narcissistic personality disorder. Individuals with narcissistic personality disorder may have special difficulties adjusting to the onset of physical and occupational limitations that are inherent in the aging process.

Gender-Related Diagnostic Issues

Of those diagnosed with narcissistic personality disorder, 50%-75% are male.

Differential Diagnosis

Other personality disorders and personality traits. Other personality disorders may be confused with narcissistic personality disorder because they have certain features in common. It is, therefore, important to distinguish among these disorders based on differences in their characteristic features. However, if an individual has personality features that meet criteria for one or more personality disorders in addition to narcissistic personality disorder, all can be diagnosed. The most useful feature in discriminating narcissistic personality disorder from histrionic, antisocial, and borderline personality disorders, in which the interactive styles are coquettish, callous, and needy, respectively, is the grandiosity characteristic of narcissistic personality disorder.

The relative stability of self-image as well as the relative lack of self-destructiveness, impulsivity, and abandonment concerns also help distinguish narcissistic personality disorder from borderline personality disorder. Excessive pride in achievements, a relative lack of emotional display, and disdain for others' sensitivities help distinguish narcissistic personality disorder from histrionic personality disorder.

Although individuals with borderline, histrionic, and narcissistic personality disorders may require much attention, those with narcissistic personality disorder specifically need that attention to be admiring. Individuals with antisocial and narcissistic personality disorders share a tendency to be tough-minded, glib, superficial, exploitative, and unempathic.

However, narcissistic personality disorder does not necessarily include characteristics of impulsivity, aggression, and deceit. In addition, individuals with antisocial personality disorder may not be as needy of the admiration and envy of others, and persons with narcissistic personality disorder usually lack the history of conduct disorder in childhood or criminal behavior in adulthood. In both narcissistic personality disorder and obsessive-compulsive personality disorder, the individual may profess a commitment to perfectionism and believe that others cannot do things as well. In contrast to the accompanying self-criticism of those with obsessive-compulsive personality disorder, individuals with narcissistic personality disorder are more likely to believe that they have achieved perfection.

Suspiciousness and social withdrawal usually distinguish those with schizotypal or paranoid personality disorder from those with narcissistic personality disorder. When these qualities are present in individuals with narcissistic personality disorder, they derive primarily from fears of having imperfections or flaws revealed.

Many highly successful individuals display personality traits that might be considered narcissistic. Only when these traits are inflexible, maladaptive, and persisting and cause significant functional impairment or subjective distress do they constitute narcissistic personality disorder.

Mania or hypomania. Grandiosity may emerge as part of manic or hypomanic episodes, but the association with mood change or functional impairments helps distinguish these episodes from narcissistic personality disorder.

Substance use disorders. Narcissistic personality disorder must also be distinguished from symptoms that may develop in association with persistent substance use.

Cluster C Personality Disorders Avoidant Personality Disorder Diagnostic Criteria 301.82 (F60.6)

A pervasive pattern of social inhibition, feelings of inadequacy, and hypersensitivity to negative evaluation, beginning by early adulthood and present in a variety of contexts, as indicated by four (or more) of the following:

1. Avoids occupational activities that involve significant interpersonal contact because of fears of criticism, disapproval, or rejection.
2. Is unwilling to get involved with people unless certain of being liked.
3. Shows restraint within intimate relationships because of the fear of being shamed or ridiculed.
4. Is preoccupied with being criticized or rejected in social situations.
5. Is inhibited in new interpersonal situations because of feelings of inadequacy.
6. Views self as socially inept, personally unappealing, or inferior to others.
7. Is unusually reluctant to take personal risks or to engage in any new activities because they may prove embarrassing.

Diagnostic Features

The essential feature of avoidant personality disorder is a pervasive pattern of social inhibition, feelings of inadequacy, and hypersensitivity to negative evaluation that begins by early adulthood and is present in a variety of contexts. Individuals with avoidant personality disorder avoid work activities that involve significant interpersonal contact because of fears of criticism, disapproval, or rejection (Criterion 1). Offers of job promotions may be declined because the new responsibilities might result in criticism from co-workers. These individuals avoid making new friends unless they are certain they will be liked and accepted without criticism (Criterion 2). Until they pass stringent tests proving the contrary, other people are assumed to be critical and disapproving. Individuals with this disorder will not join in group activities unless there are repeated and generous offers of support and nurturance.

Interpersonal intimacy is often difficult for these individuals, although they can establish intimate relationships when there is assurance of uncritical acceptance. They may act with restraint, have difficulty talking about themselves, and withhold intimate feelings for fear of being exposed, ridiculed, or shamed (Criterion 3).

Because individuals with this disorder are preoccupied with being criticized or rejected in social situations, they may have a markedly low threshold for detecting such reactions (Criterion 4). If someone is even slightly disapproving or critical, they may feel extremely hurt. They tend to be shy, quiet, inhibited, and "invisible" because of the fear that any attention would be degrading or rejecting. They expect that no matter what they say, others will see it as "wrong," and so they may say nothing at all. They react strongly to subtle cues that are suggestive of mockery or derision. Despite their longing to be active participants in social life, they fear placing their welfare in the hands of others. Individuals with avoidant personality disorder are inhibited in new interpersonal situations because they feel inadequate and have low self-esteem (Criterion 5). Doubts concerning social competence and personal appeal become especially manifest in settings involving interactions with strangers. These individuals believe themselves to be socially inept, personally unappealing, or inferior to others (Criterion 6). They are unusually reluctant to take personal risks or to engage in any new activities because these may prove embarrassing (Criterion 7). They are prone to exaggerate the potential dangers of ordinary situations, and a restricted lifestyle may result from their need for certainty and security. Someone with this disorder may cancel a job interview for fear of being embarrassed by not dressing appropriately. Marginal somatic symptoms or other problems may become the reason for avoiding new activities.

Associated Features Supporting Diagnosis

Individuals with avoidant personality disorder often vigilantly appraise the movements and expressions of those with whom they come into contact. Their fearful and tense demeanor may elicit ridicule and derision from others, which in turn confirms their self-doubts.

These individuals are very anxious about the possibility that they will react to criticism with blushing or crying. They are described by others as being "shy," "timid," "lonely," and "isolated." The major problems associated with this disorder occur in social and occupational functioning. The low self-esteem and hypersensitivity to rejection are associated with restricted interpersonal contacts. These individuals may become relatively isolated and usually do not have a large social support network that can help them weather crises. They desire affection and acceptance and may fantasize about idealized relationships with others. The avoidant behaviors can also adversely affect occupational functioning because these individuals try to avoid the types of social situations that may be important for meeting the basic demands of the job or for advancement.

Other disorders that are commonly diagnosed with avoidant personality disorder include depressive, bipolar, and anxiety disorders, especially social anxiety disorder (social phobia). Avoidant personality disorder is often diagnosed with dependent personality disorder, because individuals with avoidant personality disorder become very attached to and dependent on those few other people with whom they are friends. Avoidant personality disorder also tends to be diagnosed with borderline personality disorder and with the Cluster A personality disorders (i.e., paranoid, schizoid, or schizotypal personality disorders).

Prevalence

Data from the 2001-2002 National Epidemiologic Survey on Alcohol and Related Conditions suggest a prevalence of about 2.4% for avoidant personality disorder.

Development and Course

The avoidant behavior often starts in infancy or childhood with shyness, isolation, and fear of strangers and new situations. Although shyness in childhood is a common precursor of avoidant personality disorder, in most individuals it tends to gradually dissipate as they get older. In contrast, individuals who go on to develop avoidant personality disorder may become increasingly shy and avoidant during adolescence and early adulthood, when social relationships with new people become especially important. There is some evidence that in adults, avoidant personality disorder tends to become less evident or to remit with age. This diagnosis should be used with great caution in children and adolescents, for whom shy and avoidant behavior may be developmentally appropriate.

Gender-Related Diagnostic Issues

Avoidant personality disorder appears to be equally frequent in males and females.

Differential Diagnosis

Anxiety disorders. There appears to be a great deal of overlap between avoidant personality disorder and social anxiety disorder (social phobia), so much so that they may be alternative conceptualizations of the same or similar conditions. Avoidance also characterizes both avoidant personality disorder and agoraphobia, and they often cooccur.

Other personality disorders and personality traits. Other personality disorders may be confused with avoidant personality disorder because they have certain features in common. It is, therefore, important to distinguish among these disorders based on differences in their characteristic features. However, if an individual has personality features that meet criteria for one or more personality disorders in addition to avoidant personality disorder, all can be diagnosed. Both avoidant personality disorder and dependent personality disorder are characterized by feelings of inadequacy, hypersensitivity to criticism, and a need for reassurance. Although the primary focus of concern in avoidant personality disorder is avoidance of humiliation and rejection, in dependent personality disorder the focus is on being taken care of.

However, avoidant personality disorder and dependent personality disorder are particularly likely to co-occur. Like avoidant personality disorder, schizoid personality disorder and schizotypal personality disorder are characterized by social isolation. However, individuals with avoidant personality disorder want to have relationships with others and feel their loneliness deeply, whereas those with schizoid or schizotypal personality disorder may be content with and even prefer their social isolation. Paranoid personality disorder and avoidant personality disorder are both characterized by a reluctance to confide in others. However, in avoidant personality disorder, this reluctance is attributable more to a fear of being embarrassed or being found inadequate than to a fear of others' malicious intent.

Many individuals display avoidant personality traits. Only when these traits are inflexible, maladaptive, and persisting and cause significant functional impairment or subjective distress do they constitute avoidant personality disorder.

Personality changes due to another medical condition. Avoidant personality disorder must be distinguished from personality change due to another medical condition, in which the traits that emerge are attributable to the effects of another medical condition on the central nervous system.

Substance use disorders. Avoidant personality disorder must also be distinguished from symptoms that may develop in association with persistent substance use.

Dependent Personality Disorder Diagnostic Criteria 301.6(F60.7)

A pervasive and excessive need to be taken care of that leads to submissive and clinging behavior and fears of separation, beginning by early adulthood and present in a variety of contexts, as indicated by five (or more) of the following:

1. Has difficulty making everyday decisions without an excessive amount of advice and reassurance from others.
2. Needs others to assume responsibility for most major areas of his or her life.
3. Has difficulty expressing disagreement with others because of fear of loss of support or approval. (Note: Do not include realistic fears of retribution.)
4. Has difficulty initiating projects or doing things on his or her own (because of a lack of self-confidence in judgment or abilities rather than a lack of motivation or energy).
5. Goes to excessive lengths to obtain nurturance and support from others to the point of volunteering to do things that are unpleasant.
6. Feels uncomfortable or helpless when alone because of exaggerated fears of being unable to care for himself or herself.
7. Urgently seeks another relationship as a source of care and support when a close relationship ends.
8. Is unrealistically preoccupied with fears of being left to take care of himself or herself.
9.

Diagnostic Features

The essential feature of dependent personality disorder is a pervasive and excessive need to be taken care of that leads to submissive and clinging behavior and fears of separation. This pattern begins by early adulthood and is present in a variety of contexts. The dependent and submissive behaviors are designed to elicit caregiving and arise from a self-perception of being unable to function adequately without the help of others.

Individuals with dependent personality disorder have great difficulty making every- day decisions (e.g., what color shirt to wear to work or whether to carry an umbrella) without an excessive amount of advice and reassurance from others (Criterion 1). These individuals tend to be passive and to allow other people (often a single other person) to take the initiative and assume responsibility for most major areas of their lives (Criterion 2). Adults with this disorder typically depend on a parent or spouse to decide where they should live, what kind of job they should have, and which neighbors to befriend. Adolescents with this disorder may allow their parent(s) to decide what they should wear, with whom they should associate, how they should spend their free time, and what school or college they should attend. This need for others to assume responsibility goes beyond age appropriate and situation-appropriate requests for assistance from others (e.g., the specific needs of children, elderly persons, and handicapped persons). Dependent personality disorder may occur in an individual who has a serious medical condition or disability, but in such cases the difficulty in taking responsibility must go beyond what would normally be associated with that condition or disability.

Because they fear losing support or approval, individuals with dependent personality disorder often have difficulty expressing disagreement with other individuals, especially those on whom they are dependent (Criterion 3). These individuals feel so unable to function alone that they will agree with things that they feel are wrong rather than risk losing the help of those to whom they look for guidance. They do not get appropriately angry at others whose support and nurturance they need for fear of alienating them. If the individual's concerns regarding the consequences of expressing disagreement are realistic (e.g., realistic fears of retribution from an abusive spouse), the behavior should not be considered to be evidence of dependent personality disorder.

Individuals with this disorder have difficulty initiating projects or doing things independently (Criterion 4). They lack self-confidence and believe that they need help to begin and carry through tasks. They will wait for others to start things because they believe that as a rule others can do them better. These individuals are convinced that they are incapable of functioning independently and present themselves as inept and requiring constant assistance. They are, however, likely to function adequately if given the assurance that someone else is supervising and approving. There may be a fear of becoming or appearing to be more competent, because they may believe that this will lead to abandonment. Because they rely on others to handle their problems, they often do not learn the skills of independent living, thus perpetuating dependency.

Individuals with dependent personality disorder may go to excessive lengths to obtain nurturance and support from others, even to the point of volunteering for unpleasant tasks if such behavior will bring the care they need (Criterion 5). They are willing to submit to what others want, even if the demands are unreasonable. Their need to maintain an important bond will often result in imbalanced or distorted relationships. They may make extraordinary self-sacrifices or tolerate verbal, physical, or sexual abuse. (It should be noted that this behavior should be considered evidence of dependent personality disorder only when it can clearly be established that other options are available to the individual.) Individuals with this disorder feel uncomfortable or helpless when alone, because of their exaggerated fears of being unable to care for themselves (Criterion 6). They will "tag along" with important others just to avoid being alone, even if they are not interested or involved in what is happening.

When a close relationship ends (e.g., a breakup with a lover; the death of a caregiver), individuals with dependent personality disorder may urgently seek another relationship to provide the care and support they need (Criterion 7). Their belief that they are unable to function in the absence of a close relationship motivates these individuals to become quickly and indiscriminately attached to another individual. Individuals with this disorder are often preoccupied with fears of being left to care for themselves (Criterion 8). They see themselves as so totally dependent on the advice and help of an important other person that they worry about being abandoned by that person when there are no grounds to justify such fears. To be considered as evidence of this criterion, the fears must be excessive and unrealistic. For example, an elderly man with cancer who moves into his son's household for care is exhibiting dependent behavior that is appropriate given this person's life circumstances.

Associated Features Supporting Diagnosis

Individuals with dependent personality disorder are often characterized by pessimism and self-doubt, tend to belittle their abilities and assets, and may constantly refer to themselves as "stupid." They take criticism and disapproval as proof of their worthlessness and lose faith in themselves. They may seek overprotection and dominance from others. Occupational functioning may be impaired if independent initiative is required. They may avoid positions of responsibility and become anxious when faced with decisions. Social relations tend to be limited to those few people on whom the individual is dependent. There may be an increased risk of depressive disorders, anxiety disorders, and adjustment disorders. Dependent personality disorder often co-occurs with other personality disorders, especially borderline, avoidant, and histrionic personality disorders.

Chronic physical illness or separation anxiety disorder in childhood or adolescence may predispose the individual to the development of this disorder.

Prevalence

Data from the 2001-2002 National Epidemiologic Survey on Alcohol and Related Conditions yielded an estimated prevalence of dependent personality disorder of 0.49%, and dependent personality was estimated, based on a probability subsample from Part II of the National Comorbidity Survey Replication, to be 0.6%.

Development and Course

This diagnosis should be used with great caution, if at all, in children and adolescents, for whom dependent behavior may be developmentally appropriate.

Culture-Related Diagnostic issues

The degree to which dependent behaviors are considered to be appropriate varies substantially across different age and sociocultural groups. Age and cultural factors need to be considered in evaluating the diagnostic threshold of each criterion. Dependent behavior should be considered characteristic of the disorder only when it is clearly in excess of the individual's cultural norms or reflects unrealistic concerns. An emphasis on passivity, politeness, and deferential treatment is characteristic of some societies and may be misinterpreted as traits of dependent personality disorder. Similarly, societies may differentially foster and discourage dependent behavior in males and females.

Gender-Related Diagnostic Issues

In clinical settings, dependent personality disorder has been diagnosed more frequently in females, although some studies report similar prevalence rates among males and females.

Differential Diagnosis

Other mental disorders and medical conditions. Dependent personality disorder must be distinguished from dependency arising as a consequence of other mental disorders (e.g., depressive disorders, panic disorder, agoraphobia) and as a result of other medical conditions.

Other personality disorders and personality traits. Other personality disorders may be confused with dependent personality disorder because they have certain features in common. It is therefore important to distinguish among these disorders based on differences in their characteristic features. However, if an individual has personality features that meet criteria for one or more personality disorders in addition to dependent personality disorder, all can be diagnosed.

Although many personality disorders are characterized by dependent features, dependent personality disorder can be distinguished by its predominantly submissive, reactive, and clinging behavior.

Both dependent personality disorder and borderline personality disorder are characterized by fear of abandonment; however, the individual with borderline personality disorder reacts to abandonment with feelings of

emotional emptiness, rage, and demands, whereas the individual with dependent personality disorder reacts with increasing appeasement and submissiveness and urgently seeks a replacement relationship to provide caregiving and support. Borderline personality disorder can further be distinguished from dependent personality disorder by a typical pattern of unstable and intense relationships.

Individuals with histrionic personality disorder, like those with dependent personality disorder, have a strong need for reassurance and approval and may appear childlike and clinging.

However, unlike dependent personality disorder, which is characterized by self-effacing and docile behavior, histrionic personality disorder is characterized by gregarious flamboyance with active demands for attention. Both dependent personality disorder and avoidant personality disorder are characterized by feelings of inadequacy, hypersensitivity to criticism, and a need for reassurance; however, individuals with avoidant personality disorder have such a strong fear of humiliation and rejection that they withdraw until they are certain they will be accepted. In contrast, individuals with dependent personality disorder have a pattern of seeking and maintaining connections to important others, rather than avoiding and withdrawing from relationships.

Many individuals display dependent personality traits. Only when these traits are inflexible, maladaptive, and persisting and cause significant functional impairment or subjective distress do they constitute dependent personality disorder.

Personality changes due to another medical condition.

Dependent personality disorder must be distinguished from personality change due to another medical condition, in which the traits that emerge are attributable to the effects of another medical condition on the central nervous system.

Substance use disorders. Dependent personality disorder must also be distinguished from symptoms that may develop in association with persistent substance use.

Obsessive-Compulsive Personality Disorder Diagnostic Criteria 301.4 (F60.5)

A pervasive pattern of preoccupation with orderliness, perfectionism, and mental and interpersonal control, at the expense of flexibility, openness, and efficiency, beginning by early adulthood and present in a variety of contexts, as indicated by four (or more) of the following:

1. Is preoccupied with details, rules, lists, order, organization, or schedules to the extent that the major point of the activity is lost.
2. Shows perfectionism that interferes with task completion (e.g., is unable to complete a project because his or her own overly strict standards are not met).
3. Is excessively devoted to work and productivity to the exclusion of leisure activities and friendships (not accounted for by obvious economic necessity).
4. Is overconscientious, scrupulous, and inflexible about matters of morality, ethics, or values (not accounted for by cultural or religious identification).
5. Is unable to discard worn-out or worthless objects even when they have no sentimental value.
6. Is reluctant to delegate tasks or to work with others unless they submit to exactly his or her way of doing things.
7. Adopts a miserly spending style toward both self and others; money is viewed as something to be hoarded for future catastrophes.
8. Shows rigidity and stubbornness.

Diagnostic Features

The essential feature of obsessive-compulsive personality disorder is a preoccupation with orderliness, perfectionism, and mental and interpersonal control, at the expense of flexibility, openness, and efficiency. This pattern begins by early adulthood and is present in a variety of contexts.

Individuals with obsessive-compulsive personality disorder attempt to maintain a sense of control through painstaking attention to rules, trivial details, procedures, lists, schedules, or form to the extent that the major point of the activity is lost (Criterion 1). They are excessively careful and prone to repetition, paying extraordinary attention to detail and repeatedly checking for possible mistakes. They are oblivious to the fact that other people tend to become very annoyed at the delays and inconveniences that result from this behavior. For example, when such individuals misplace a list of things to be done, they will spend an inordinate amount of time looking for the list rather than spending a few moments recreating it from memory and proceeding to accomplish the tasks. Time is poorly allocated, and the most important tasks are left to the last moment. The perfectionism and self-imposed high standards of performance cause significant dysfunction and distress in these individuals. They may become so involved in making every detail of a project absolutely perfect that the project is never finished (Criterion 2). For example, the completion of a written report is delayed by numerous time-consuming rewrites that all come up short of "perfection." Deadlines are missed, and aspects of the individual's life that are not the current focus of activity may fall into disarray.

Individuals with obsessive-compulsive personality disorder display excessive devotion to work and productivity to the exclusion of leisure activities and friendships (Criterion 3). This behavior is not accounted for by economic necessity. They often feel that they do not have time to take an evening or a weekend day off to go on an outing or to just relax. They may keep postponing a pleasurable activity, such as a vacation, so that it may never occur. When they do take time for leisure activities or vacations, they are very uncomfortable unless they have taken along something to work on, so they do not "waste time." There may be a great concentration on household chores (e.g., repeated excessive cleaning so that "one could eat off the floor"). If they spend time with friends, it is likely to be in some kind of formally organized activity (e.g., sports). Hobbies or recreational activities are approached as serious tasks requiring careful organization and hard work to master. The emphasis is on perfect performance. These individuals turn play into a structured task (e.g., correcting an infant for not putting rings on the post in the right order; telling a toddler to ride his or her tricycle in a straight line; turning a baseball game into a harsh "lesson").

Individuals with obsessive-compulsive personality disorder may be excessively conscientious, scrupulous, and inflexible about matters of morality, ethics, or values (Criterion 4). They may force themselves and others to follow rigid moral principles and very strict standards of performance. They may also be mercilessly self-critical about their own mistakes. Individuals with this disorder are rigidly deferential to authority and rules and insist on quite literal compliance, with no rule bending for extenuating circumstances. For example, the individual will not lend a quarter to a friend who needs one to make a telephone call because "neither a borrower nor a lender be" or because it would be "bad" for the person's character. These qualities should not be accounted for by the individual's cultural or religious identification.

Individuals with this disorder may be unable to discard worn out or worthless objects, even when they have no sentimental value (Criterion 5). Often these individuals will admit to being "pack rats." They regard discarding objects as wasteful because "you never know when you might need something" and will become upset if someone tries to get rid of the things they have saved. Their spouses or roommates may complain about the amount of space taken up by old parts, magazines, broken appliances, and so on.

Individuals with obsessive-compulsive personality disorder are reluctant to delegate tasks or to work with others (Criterion 6). They stubbornly and unreasonably insist that everything be done their way and that people conform to their way of doing things. They often give very detailed instructions about how things should be done (e.g., there is one and only one way to mow the lawn, wash the dishes, build a doghouse) and are surprised and irritated if others suggest creative alternatives. At other times they may reject offers of help even when behind schedule because they believe no one else can do it right.

Individuals with this disorder may be miserly and stingy and maintain a standard of living far below what they can afford, believing that spending must be tightly controlled to provide for future catastrophes (Criterion 7). Obsessive-compulsive personality disorder is characterized by rigidity and stubbornness (Criterion 8). Individuals with this disorder are so concerned about having things done the one "correct" way that they have trouble going along with anyone else's ideas. These individuals plan ahead in meticulous detail and are unwilling to consider changes. Totally wrapped up in their own perspective, they have difficulty acknowledging the viewpoints of others. Friends and colleagues may become frustrated by this constant rigidity. Even when individuals with obsessive-compulsive personality disorder recognize that it may be in their interest to compromise, they may stubbornly refuse to do so, arguing that it is "the principle of the thing."

Associated Features Supporting Diagnosis

When rules and established procedures do not dictate the correct answer, decision making may become a time-consuming, often painful process.

Individuals with obsessive- compulsive personality disorder may have such difficulty deciding which tasks take priority or what is the best way of doing some particular tasks that they may never get started on anything. They are prone to become upset or angry in situations in which they are not able to maintain control of their physical or interpersonal environment, although the anger is typically not expressed directly. For example, an individual may be angry when service in a restaurant is poor, but instead of complaining to the management, the individual ruminates about how much to leave as a tip. On other occasions, anger may be expressed with righteous indignation over a seemingly minor matter. Individuals with this disorder may be especially attentive to their relative status in dominance-submission relationships and may display excessive deference to an authority they respect and excessive resistance to authority they do not respect.

Individuals with this disorder usually express affection in a highly controlled or stilted fashion and may be very uncomfortable in the presence of others who are emotionally expressive. Their everyday relationships have a formal and serious quality, and they may be stiff in situations in which others would smile and be happy (e.g., greeting a lover at the airport). They carefully hold themselves back until they are sure that whatever they say will be perfect. They may be preoccupied with logic and intellect, and intolerant of affective behavior in others. They often have difficulty expressing tender feelings, rarely paying compliments.

Individuals with this disorder may experience occupational difficulties and distress, particularly when confronted with new situations that demand flexibility and compromise. Individuals with anxiety disorders, including generalized anxiety disorder, social anxiety disorder (social phobia), and specific phobias, and obsessive- compulsive disorder (OCD) have an increased likelihood of having a personality disturbance that meets criteria for obsessive-compulsive personality disorder. Even so, it appears that the majority of individuals with OCD do not have a pattern of behavior that meets criteria for this personality disorder. Many of the features of obsessive- compulsive personality disorder overlap with "type A" personality characteristics (e.g., preoccupation with work, competitiveness, time urgency), and these features may be present in people at risk for myocardial infarction. There may be an association between obsessive- compulsive personality disorder and depressive and bipolar disorders and eating disorders.

Prevalence

Obsessive-compulsive personality disorder is one of the most prevalent personality disorders in the general population, with estimated prevalence ranging from 2.1% to 7.9%.

Culture-Related Diagnostic Issues

In assessing an individual for obsessive-compulsive personality disorder, the clinician should not include those behaviors that reflect habits, customs, or interpersonal styles that are culturally sanctioned by the individual's reference group. Certain cultures place substantial emphasis on work and productivity; the resulting behaviors in members of those societies need not be considered indications of obsessive-compulsive personality disorder.

Gender-Related Diagnostic Issues

In systematic studies, obsessive-compulsive personality disorder appears to be diagnosed about twice as often among males.

Differential Diagnosis

Obsessive-compulsive disorder. Despite the similarity in names, OCD is usually easily distinguished from obsessive-compulsive personality disorder by the presence of true obsessions and compulsions in OCD. When criteria for both obsessive-compulsive personality disorder and OCD are met, both diagnoses should be recorded.

Hoarding disorder. A diagnosis of hoarding disorder should be considered especially when hoarding is extreme (e.g., accumulated stacks of worthless objects present a fire hazard and make it difficult for others to walk through the house). When criteria for both obsessive-compulsive personality disorder and hoarding disorder are met, both diagnoses should be recorded.

Other personality disorders and personality traits.

Other personality disorders may be confused with obsessive-compulsive personality disorder because they have certain features in common. It is, therefore, important to distinguish among these disorders based on differences in their characteristic features. However, if an individual has personality features that meet criteria for one or more personality disorders in addition to obsessive-compulsive personality disorder, all can be diagnosed. Individuals with narcissistic personality disorder may also profess a commitment to perfectionism and believe that others cannot do things as well, but these individuals are more likely to believe that they have achieved perfection, whereas those with obsessive- compulsive personality disorder are usually self-critical. Individuals with narcissistic or antisocial personality disorder lack generosity but will indulge themselves, whereas those with obsessive-compulsive personality disorder adopt a miserly spending style toward both self and others. Both schizoid personality disorder and obsessive-compulsive personality disorder may be characterized by an apparent formality and social detachment. In obsessive-compulsive personality disorder, this stems from discomfort with emotions and excessive devotion to work, whereas in schizoid personality disorder there is a fundamental lack of capacity for intimacy.

Obsessive-compulsive personality traits in moderation may be especially adaptive, particularly in situations that reward high performance. Only when these traits are inflexible, maladaptive, and persisting and cause significant functional impairment or subjective distress do they constitute obsessive-compulsive personality disorder.

Personality changes due to another medical condition. Obsessive- compulsive personality disorder must be distinguished from personality change due to another medical condition, in which the traits emerge attributable to the effects of another medical condition on the central nervous system.

Substance use disorders. Obsessive-compulsive personality disorder must also be distinguished from symptoms that may develop in association with persistent substance use.

Paraphilic Disorders

Paraphilic disorders included in this section are voyeuristic disorder (spying on others in private activities), exhibitionistic disorder (exposing the genitals), frotteuristic disorder (touching or rubbing against a nonconsenting individual), sexual masochism disorder (undergoing humiliation, bondage, or suffering), sexual sadism disorder (inflicting humiliation, bondage, or suffering), pedophilic disorder (sexual focus on children), fetishistic disorder (using nonliving objects or having a highly specific focus on nongenital body parts), and transvestic disorder (engaging in sexually arousing crossdressing). These disorders have traditionally been selected for specific listing and assignment of explicit diagnostic criteria in DSM for two main reasons: they are relatively common, in relation to other paraphilic disorders, and some of them entail actions for their satisfaction that, because of their noxiousness or potential harm to others, are classed as criminal offenses. The eight listed disorders do not exhaust the list of possible paraphilic disorders. Many dozens of distinct paraphilias have been identified and named, and almost any of them could, by virtue of its negative consequences for the individual or for others, rise to the level of a paraphilic disorder. The diagnoses of the other specified and unspecified paraphilic disorders are therefore indispensable and will be required in many cases.

In this section, the order of presentation of the listed paraphilic disorders generally corresponds to common classification schemes for these conditions. The first group of disorders is based on anomalous activity preferences. These disorders are subdivided into courtship disorders, which resemble distorted components of human courtship behavior (voyeuristic disorder, exhibitionistic disorder, and frotteuristic disorder), and algolagnic disorders, which involve pain and suffering (sexual masochism disorder and sexual sadism disorder). The second group of disorders is based on anomalous target preferences. These disorders include one directed at other humans (pedophilic disorder) and two directed elsewhere (fetishistic disorder and transvestic disorder).

The term paraphilia denotes any intense and persistent sexual interest other than sexual interest in genital stimulation or preparatory fondling with phenotypically normal, physically mature, consenting human partners. In some circumstances, the criteria "intense and persistent" may be difficult to apply, such as in the assessment of persons who are very old or medically ill and who may not have "intense" sexual interests of any kind. In such circumstances, the term paraphilia may be defined as any sexual interest greater than or equal to normophilic sexual interests. There are also specific paraphilias that are generally better described as preferential sexual interests than as intense sexual interests.

Some paraphilias primarily concern the individual's erotic activities, and others primarily concern the individual's erotic targets. Examples of the former would include intense and persistent interests in spanking, whipping, cutting, binding, or strangulating another person, or an interest in these activities that equals or exceeds the individual's interest in copulation or equivalent interaction with another person. Examples of the latter would include intense or preferential sexual interest in children, corpses, or amputees (as a class), as well as intense or preferential interest in nonhuman animals, such as horses or dogs, or in inanimate objects, such as shoes or articles made of rubber.

A paraphilic disorder is a paraphilia that is currently causing distress or impairment to the individual or a paraphilia whose satisfaction has entailed personal harm, or risk of harm, to others. A paraphilia is a necessary but not a sufficient condition for having a paraphilic disorder, and a paraphilia by itself does not necessarily justify or require clinical intervention.

In the diagnostic criteria set for each of the listed paraphilic disorders. Criterion A specifies the qualitative nature of the paraphilia (e.g., an erotic focus on children or on exposing the genitals to strangers), and Criterion B specifies the negative consequences of the paraphilia (i.e., distress, impairment, or harm to others). In keeping with the distinction between paraphilias and paraphilic disorders, the term diagnosis should be reserved for individuals who meet both Criteria A and B (i.e., individuals who have a paraphilic disorder). If an individual meets Criterion A but not Criterion B for a particular paraphilia—a circumstance that might arise when a benign paraphilia is discovered during the clinical investigation of some other condition— then the individual may be said to have that paraphilia but not a paraphilic disorder.

It is not rare for an individual to manifest two or more paraphilias. In some cases, the paraphilic foci are closely related and the connection between the paraphilias is intuitively comprehensible (e.g., foot fetishism and shoe fetishism). In other cases, the connection between the paraphilias is not obvious, and the presence of multiple paraphilias may be coincidental or else related to some generalized vulnerability to anomalies of psychosexual development. In any event, comorbid diagnoses of separate paraphilic disorders may be warranted if more than one paraphilia is causing suffering to the individual or harm to others.

Because of the two-pronged nature of diagnosing paraphilic disorders, clinician-rated or self-rated measures and severity assessments could address either the strength of the paraphilia itself or the seriousness of its consequences. Although the distress and impairment stipulated in the Criterion B are special in being the immediate or ultimate result of the paraphilia and not primarily the result of some other factor, the phenomena of reactive depression, anxiety, guilt, poor work history, impaired social relations, and so on are not unique in themselves and may be quantified with multipurpose measures of psychosocial functioning or quality of life.

The most widely applicable framework for assessing the strength of a paraphilia itself is one in which examinees' paraphilic sexual fantasies, urges, or behaviors are evaluated in relation to their normophilic sexual interests and behaviors. In a clinical interview or on self-administered questionnaires, examinees can be asked whether their paraphilic sexual fantasies, urges, or behaviors are weaker than, approximately equal to, or stronger than their normophilic sexual interests and behaviors. This same type of comparison can be, and usually is, employed in psychophysiological measures of sexual interest, such as penile plethysmography in males or viewing time in males and females.

Voyeuristic Disorder

Diagnostic Criteria 302.82 (F65.3)

- Over a period of at least 6 months, recurrent and intense sexual arousal from observing an unsuspecting person who is naked, in the process of disrobing, or engaging in sexual activity, as manifested by fantasies, urges, or behaviors.

- The individual has acted on these sexual urges with a nonconsenting person, or the sexual urges or fantasies cause clinically significant distress or impairment in social, occupational,

or other important areas of functioning. The individual experiencing
the arousal and/or acting on the urges is at least 18 years of age.

Specify if: In a controlled environment: This specifier is primarily applicable
to individuals living in institutional or other settings where opportunities to
engage in voyeuristic behavior are restricted.

In full remission: The individual has not acted on the urges with a
nonconsenting person, and there has been no distress or impairment in social,
occupational, or other areas of functioning, for at least 5 years while in an
uncontrolled environment.

Specifiers: The "in full remission" specifier does not address the continued
presence or absence of voyeurism per se, which may still be present after
behaviors and distress have remitted.

Diagnostic Features

The diagnostic criteria for voyeuristic disorder can apply both to individuals
who more or less freely disclose this paraphilic interest and to those who
categorically deny any sexual arousal from observing an unsuspecting person
who is naked, disrobing, or engaged in sexual activity despite substantial
objective evidence to the contrary. If disclosing individuals also report distress
or psychosocial problems because of their voyeuristic sexual preferences, they
could be diagnosed with voyeuristic disorder. On the other hand, if they declare
no distress, demonstrated by lack of anxiety, obsessions, guilt, or shame, about
these paraphilic impulses and are not impaired in other important areas of
functioning because of this sexual interest, and their psychiatric or legal
histories indicate that they do not act on it, they could be ascertained as having
voyeuristic sexual interest but should not be diagnosed with voyeuristic
disorder.

Nondisclosing individuals include, for example, individuals known to have
been spying repeatedly on unsuspecting persons who are naked or engaging
in sexual activity on separate occasions but who deny any urges or fantasies
concerning such sexual behavior, and who may report that known episode of
watching unsuspecting naked or sexually active persons were all accidental and
nonsexual. Others may disclose past episodes of observing unsuspecting naked
or sexually active persons but contest any significant or sustained sexual interest
in this behavior. Since these individuals deny having fantasies or impulses about

watching others nude or involved in sexual activity, it follows that they would also reject feeling subjectively distressed or socially impaired by such impulses. Despite their nondisclosing stance, such individuals may be diagnosed with voyeuristic disorder. Recurrent voyeuristic behavior constitutes sufficient support for voyeurism (by fulfilling Criterion A) and simultaneously demonstrates that this paraphilically motivated behavior is causing harm to others (by fulfilling Criterion B).

"Recurrent" spying on unsuspecting persons who are naked or engaging in sexual activity (i.e., multiple victims, each on a separate occasion) may, as a general rule, be interpreted as three or more victims on separate occasions. Fewer victims can be interpreted as satisfying this criterion if there were multiple occasions of watching the same victim or if there is corroborating evidence of a distinct or preferential interest in secret watching of naked or sexually active unsuspecting persons. Note that multiple victims, as suggested earlier, are a sufficient but not a necessary condition for diagnosis; the criteria may also be met if the individual acknowledges intense voyeuristic sexual interest.

The Criterion A time frame, indicating that signs or symptoms of voyeurism must have persisted for at least 6 months, should also be understood as a general guideline, not a strict threshold, to ensure that the sexual interest in secretly watching unsuspecting naked or sexually active others is not merely transient. Adolescence and puberty generally increase sexual curiosity and activity. To alleviate the risk of pathologizing normative sexual interest and behavior during pubertal adolescence, the minimum age for the diagnosis of voyeuristic disorder is 18 years (Criterion C).

Prevalence

Voyeuristic acts are the most common of potentially law-breaking sexual behaviors. The population prevalence of voyeuristic disorder is unknown. However, based on voyeuristic sexual acts in nonclinical samples, the highest possible lifetime prevalence for voyeuristic disorder is approximately 12% in males and 4% in females.

Development and Course

Adult males with voyeuristic disorder often first become aware of their sexual interest in secretly watching unsuspecting persons during adolescence. However, the minimum age for a diagnosis of voyeuristic disorder is 18 years because there is substantial difficulty in differentiating it from age-appropriate puberty-related sexual curiosity and activity. The persistence of voyeurism over time is unclear.

Voyeuristic disorder, however, per definition requires one or more contributing factors that may change over time with or without treatment: subjective distress (e.g., guilt, shame, intense sexual frustration, loneliness), psychiatric morbidity, hypersexuality, and sexual impulsivity; psychosocial impairment; and/or the propensity to act out sexually by spying on unsuspecting naked or sexually active persons. Therefore, the course of voyeuristic disorder is likely to vary with age.

Risk and Prognostic Factors

Temperamental. Voyeurism is a necessary precondition for voyeuristic disorder; hence, risk factors for voyeurism should also increase the rate of voyeuristic disorder.

Environmental. Childhood sexual abuse, substance misuse, and sexual preoccupation/ hypersexuality have been suggested as risk factors, although the causal relationship to voyeurism is uncertain and the specificity unclear.

Gender-Related Diagnostic Issues

Voyeuristic disorder is very uncommon among females in clinical settings, while the male-to-female ratio for single sexually arousing voyeuristic acts might be 3:1.

Differential Diagnosis

Conduct disorder and antisocial personality disorder. Conduct disorder in adolescents and antisocial personality disorder would be characterized by additional norm-breaking and antisocial behaviors, and the specific sexual interest in secretly watching unsuspecting others who are naked or engaging in sexual activity should be lacking.

Substance use disorders. Substance use disorders might involve single voyeuristic episodes by intoxicated individuals but should not involve the typical sexual interest in secretly watching unsuspecting persons being naked or engaging in sexual activity. Hence, recurrent voyeuristic sexual fantasies, urges, or behaviors that occur also when the individual is not intoxicated suggest that voyeuristic disorder might be present.

Comorbidity

Known comorbidities in voyeuristic disorder are largely based on research with males suspected of or convicted for acts involving the secret watching of unsuspecting nude or sexually active persons.

Hence, these comorbidities might not apply to all individuals with voyeuristic disorder. Conditions that occur comorbidly with voyeuristic disorder include hypersexuality and other paraphilic disorders, particularly exhibitionistic disorder. Depressive, bipolar, anxiety, and substance use

disorders; attention-deficit/hyperactivity disorder; and conduct disorder and antisocial personality disorder are also frequent co-morbid conditions.

Pedophilic Disorder

Diagnostic Criteria 302.2 (F65.4)

i. Over a period of at least 6 months, recurrent, intense sexually arousing fantasies, sexual urges, or behaviors involving sexual activity with a prepubescent child or children (generally age 13 years or younger).

ii. The individual has acted on these sexual urges, or the sexual urges or fantasies cause marked distress or interpersonal difficulty.

iii. The individual is at least age 16 years and at least 5 years older than the child or children in Criterion A. Note: Do not include an individual in late adolescence involved in an ongoing sexual relationship with a 12-or 13-year-old. Specify whether: Exclusive type (attracted only to children)

Nonexclusive type Specify if:

Sexually attracted to males

Sexually attracted to females

Sexually attracted to both Specify if:

Limited to incest Diagnostic Features

The diagnostic criteria for pedophilic disorder are intended to apply both to individuals who freely disclose this paraphilia and to individuals who deny any sexual attraction to prepubertal children (generally age 13 years or younger), despite substantial objective evidence to the contrary. Examples of disclosing this paraphilia include candidly acknowledging an intense sexual interest in children and indicating that sexual interest in children is greater than or equal to sexual interest in physically mature individuals. If individuals also complain that their sexual attractions or preferences for children are causing psychosocial difficulties, they may be diagnosed with pedophilic disorder. However, if they report an absence of feelings of guilt, shame, or anxiety about these impulses and are not functionally limited by their paraphilic impulses (according to self-report, objective assessment, or both), and their self-reported and legally recorded histories indicate that they have never acted on their impulses, then these individuals have a pedophilic sexual orientation but not pedophilic disorder.

Examples of individuals who deny attraction to children include individuals who are known to have sexually approached multiple children on separate occasions but who deny any urges or fantasies about sexual behavior involving children, and who may further claim that the known episodes of physical contact were all unintentional and nonsexual. Other individuals may acknowledge past episodes of sexual behavior involving children but deny any significant or sustained sexual interest in children. Since these individuals may deny experiences impulses or fantasies involving children, they may also deny feeling subjectively distressed. Such individuals may still be diagnosed with pedophilic disorder despite the absence of self-reported distress, provided that there is evidence of recurrent behaviors persisting for 6 months (Criterion A) and evidence that the individual has acted on sexual urges or experienced interpersonal difficulties as a consequence of the disorder (Criterion B).

Presence of multiple victims, as discussed above, is sufficient but not necessary for diagnosis; that is, the individual can still meet Criterion A by merely acknowledging intense or preferential sexual interest in children.

The Criterion A clause, indicating that the signs or symptoms of pedophilia have persisted for 6 months or longer, is intended to ensure that the sexual attraction to children is not merely transient. However, the diagnosis may be made if there is clinical evidence of sustained persistence of the sexual attraction to children even if the 6month duration can- not be precisely determined.

Associated Features Supporting Diagnosis

The extensive use of pornography depicting prepubescent children is a useful diagnostic indicator of pedophilic disorder. This is a specific instance of the general case that individuals are likely to choose the kind of pornography that corresponds to their sexual interests.

Prevalence

The population prevalence of pedophilic disorder is unknown. The highest possible prevalence for pedophilic disorder in the male population is approximately 3%-5%. The population prevalence of pedophilic disorder in females is even more uncertain, but it is likely a small fraction of the prevalence in males.

Development and Course

Adult males with pedophilic disorder may indicate that they become aware of strong or preferential sexual interest in children around the time of puberty—the same time frame in which males who later prefer physically mature partners became aware of their sexual interest in women or men. Attempting to diagnose pedophilic disorder at the age at which it first manifests is problematic because of the difficulty during adolescent development in differentiating it from age-appropriate sexual interest in peers or from sexual curiosity. Hence, Criterion C requires for diagnosis a minimum age of 16 years and at least 5 years older than the child or children in Criterion A.

Pedophilia per se appears to be a lifelong condition. Pedophilic disorder, however, necessarily includes other elements that may change over time with or without treatment: subjective distress (e.g., guilt, shame, intense sexual frustration, or feelings of isolation) or psychosocial impairment, or the propensity to act out sexually with children, or both. Therefore, the course of pedophilic disorder may fluctuate, increase, or decrease with age.

Adults with pedophilic disorder may report an awareness of sexual interest in children that preceded engaging in sexual behavior involving children or self-identification as a pedophile. Advanced age is as likely to similarly diminish the frequency of sexual behavior involving children as it does other paraphilically motivated and normophilic sexual behavior.

Risk and Prognostic Factors

Temperamental. There appears to be an interaction between pedophilia and antisociality, such that males with both traits are more likely to act out sexually with children. Thus, antisocial personality disorder may be considered a risk factor for pedophilic disorder in males with pedophilia.

Environmental. Adult males with pedophilia often report that they were sexually abused as children. It is unclear, however, whether this correlation reflects a causal influence of childhood sexual abuse on adult pedophilia.

Genetic and physiological. Since pedophilia is a necessary condition for pedophilic disorder, any factor that increases the probability of pedophilia also increases the risk of pedophilic disorder. There is some evidence that neurodevelopmental perturbation in utero increases the probability of development of a pedophilic orientation.

Gender-Related Diagnostic Issues

Psychophysiological laboratory measures of sexual interest, which are sometimes useful in diagnosing pedophilic disorder in males, are not necessarily useful in diagnosing this disorder in females, even when an identical procedure (e.g., viewing time) or analogous procedures (e.g., penile plethysmography and vaginal photoplethysmography) are available.

Diagnostic Markers

Psychophysiological measures of sexual interest may sometimes be useful when an individual's history suggests the possible presence of pedophilic disorder, but the individual denies strong or preferential attraction to children. The most thoroughly researched and longest used of such measures is penile plethysmography, although the sensitivity and specificity of diagnosis may vary from one site to another. Viewing time, using photographs of nude or minimally clothed persons as visual stimuli, is also used to diagnose pedophilic disorder, especially in combination with self-report measures. Mental health professionals in the United States, however, should be aware that possession of such visual stimuli, even for diagnostic purposes, may violate American law regarding possession of child pornography and leave the mental health professional susceptible to criminal prosecution.

Differential Diagnosis

Many of the conditions that could be differential diagnoses for pedophilic disorder also sometimes occur as comorbid diagnoses. It is therefore generally necessary to evaluate the evidence for pedophilic disorder and other possible conditions as separate questions.

Antisocial personality disorder. This disorder increases the likelihood that a person who is primarily attracted to the mature physique will approach a child, on one or a few occasions, on the basis of relative availability. The individual often shows other signs of this personality disorder, such as recurrent law breaking.

Alcohol and substance use disorders. The disinhibiting effects of intoxication may also increase the likelihood that a person who is primarily attracted to the mature physique will sexually approach a child.

Obsessive-compulsive disorder. There are occasional individuals who complain about ego-dystonic thoughts and worries about possible attraction to children. Clinical interviewing usually reveals an absence of sexual thoughts about children during high states of sexual arousal (e.g., approaching orgasm during masturbation) and sometimes additional ego-dystonic, intrusive sexual ideas (e.g., concerns about homosexuality).

Comorbidity

Psychiatric comorbidity of pedophilic disorder includes substance use disorders; depressive, bipolar, and anxiety disorders; antisocial personality disorder; and other paraphilic disorders. However, findings on comorbid disorders are largely among individuals convicted for sexual offenses involving children (almost all males) and may not be generalizable to other individuals with pedophilic disorder (e.g., individuals who have never approached a child sexually but who qualify for the diagnosis of pedophilic disorder on the basis of subjective distress).

Trauma and Stress Disorders

Trauma and Stress disorders include disorders in which exposure to a traumatic or stressful event is listed explicitly as a diagnostic criterion. These include reactive attachment disorder, disinhibited social engagement disorder, posttraumatic stress disorder (PTSD), acute stress disorder, and adjustment disorders. Placement of this section reflects the close relationship between these diagnoses and disorders in the surrounding chapters on anxiety disorders, obsessive-compulsive and related disorders, and dissociative disorders.

Psychological distress following exposure to a traumatic or stressful event is quite variable. In some cases, symptoms can be well understood within an anxiety or fear-based context. It is clear, however, that many individuals who have been exposed to a traumatic or stressful event exhibit a phenotype in which, rather than anxiety or fear-based symptoms, the most prominent clinical characteristics are anhedonic and dysphoric symptoms, externalizing angry and aggressive symptoms, or dissociative symptoms. Because of these variable expressions of clinical distress following exposure to catastrophic or aversive events, the aforementioned disorders have been grouped under a separate category: trauma- and stressor-related disorders. Furthermore, it is not uncommon for the clinical picture to include some combination of the above symptoms (with or without anxiety or fear-based symptoms). Such a heterogeneous picture has long been recognized in adjustment disorders, as well. Social neglect— that is, the absence of adequate caregiving during childhood—is a diagnostic requirement of both reactive attachment disorder and disinhibited social engagement disorder. Although the two disorders share a common etiology, the former is expressed as an internalizing disorder with depressive symptoms and with- drawn behavior, while the latter is marked by disinhibition and externalizing behavior.

Trauma and Stress disorders are new to the DSM-5. These disorders are caused by extreme overwhelming events. Trauma and stress disorders include posttraumatic stress disorder, acute stress disorder, and adjustment disorder.

Posttraumatic Stress Disorder Diagnostic Criteria 309.81 (F43.10)

Posttraumatic Stress Disorder Note: The following criteria apply to adults, adolescents, and children older than 6 years. For children 6 years and younger, see corresponding criteria below.

- Exposure to actual or threatened death, serious injury, or sexual violence in one (or more) of the following ways:

- Directly experiencing the traumatic event(s).

- Witnessing, in person, the event(s) as it occurred to others.

- Learning that the traumatic event(s) occurred to a close family member or close friend. In cases of actual or threatened death of a family member or friend, the event(s) must have been violent or accidental.

- Experiencing repeated or extreme exposure to aversive details of the traumatic event(s) (e.g., first responders collecting human remains: police officers repeatedly exposed to details of child abuse).

Note: Criterion A4 does not apply to exposure through electronic media, television, movies, or pictures, unless this exposure is work related.

- Presence of one (or more) of the following intrusion symptoms associated with the traumatic event(s), beginning after the traumatic event(s) occurred:

1. Recurrent, involuntary, and intrusive distressing memories of the traumatic event(s). Note: In children older than 6 years, repetitive play may occur in which themes or aspects of the traumatic event(s) are expressed.
2. Recurrent distressing dreams in which the content and/or effect of the dream are related to the traumatic event(s). Note: In children, there may be frightening dreams without recognizable content.
3. Dissociative reactions (e.g., flashbacks) in which the individual feels or acts as if the traumatic event(s) were recurring. (Such reactions

may occur on a continuum, with the most extreme expression being a complete loss of awareness of present surroundings.) Note: In children, trauma-specific reenactment may occur in play.

4. Intense or prolonged psychological distress at exposure to internal or external cues that symbolize or resemble an aspect of the traumatic event(s).

5. Marked physiological reactions to internal or external cues that symbolize or resemble an aspect of the traumatic event(s).

6. Persistent avoidance of stimuli associated with the traumatic event(s), beginning after the traumatic event(s) occurred, as evidenced by one or both of the following:

7. Avoidance of or efforts to avoid distressing memories, thoughts, or feelings about or closely associated with the traumatic event(s).

8. Avoidance of or efforts to avoid external reminders (people, places, conversations, activities, objects, situations) that arouse distressing memories, thoughts, or feelings about or closely associated with the traumatic event(s).

9. Negative alterations in cognitions and mood associated with the traumatic event(s), beginning, or worsening after the traumatic event(s) occurred, as evidenced by two (or more) of the following:

10. Inability to remember an important aspect of the traumatic event(s) (typically due to dissociative amnesia and not to other factors such as head injury, alcohol, or drugs).

• Persistent and exaggerated negative beliefs or expectations about oneself, others, or the world (e.g., "I am bad," "No one can be trusted," 'The world is completely dangerous," "My whole nervous system is permanently ruined").

• Persistent, distorted cognitions about the cause or consequences of the traumatic event(s) that lead the individual to blame himself/herself or others.

• Persistent negative emotional state (e.g., fear, horror, anger, guilt, or shame).

• Markedly diminished interest or participation in significant activities.

• Feelings of detachment or estrangement from others.

• Persistent inability to experience positive emotions (e.g., inability to experience happiness, satisfaction, or loving feelings).

• Marked alterations in arousal and reactivity associated with the traumatic event(s), beginning, or worsening after the traumatic event(s) occurred, as evidenced by two (or more) of the following:

• Irritable behavior and angry outbursts (with little or no provocation) typically expressed as verbal or physical aggression toward people or objects.

• Reckless or self-destructive behavior.

• Hypervigilance.

• Exaggerated startle response.

• Problems with concentration.

• Sleep disturbance (e.g., difficulty falling or staying asleep or restless sleep).

• Duration of the disturbance (Criteria B, C, D, and E) is more than 1 month.

• The disturbance causes clinically significant distress or impairment in social, occupational, or other important areas of functioning.

• The disturbance is not attributable to the physiological effects of a substance (e.g., medication, alcohol) or another medical condition.

Specify whether:

With dissociative symptoms: The individual's symptoms meet the criteria for posttraumatic stress disorder, and in addition, in response to the stressor, the individual experiences persistent or recurrent symptoms of either of the following:

- Depersonalization: Persistent or recurrent experiences of feeling detached from, and as if one were an outside observer of, one's mental processes or body (e.g., feeling as though one were in a dream; feeling a sense of unreality of self or body or of time moving slowly).

- Derealization: Persistent or recurrent experiences of unreality of surroundings (e.g., the world around the individual is experienced as unreal, dreamlike, distant, or distorted).

Note: To use this subtype, the dissociative symptoms must not be attributable to the physiological effects of a substance (e.g., blackouts, behavior during alcohol intoxication) or another medical condition (e.g., complex partial seizures).

Specify if:

With delayed expression: If the full diagnostic criteria are not met until at least 6 months after the event (although the onset and expression of some symptoms may be immediate).

Posttraumatic Stress Disorder for Children 6 Years and Younger

- In children 6 years and younger, exposure to actual or threatened death, serious injury, or sexual violence in one (or more) of the following ways:

- Directly experiencing the traumatic event(s).

- Witnessing, in person, the event(s) as it occurred to others, especially primary caregivers.

Note: Witnessing does not include events that are witnessed only in electronic media, television, movies, or pictures.

•

• Learning that the traumatic event(s) occurred to a parent or caregiving figure.

• Presence of one (or more) of the following intrusion symptoms associated with the traumatic event(s), beginning after the traumatic event(s) occurred:

1. Recurrent, involuntary, and intrusive distressing memories of the traumatic event(s).
2. Note: Spontaneous and intrusive memories may not necessarily appear distressing and may be expressed as play reenactment.
3. Recurrent distressing dreams in which the content and/or effect of the dream are related to the traumatic event(s).
4. Note: It may not be possible to ascertain that the frightening content is related to the traumatic event.

Dissociative reactions (e.g., flashbacks) in which the child feels or acts as if the traumatic event(s) were recurring. (Such reactions may occur on a continuum, with the most extreme expression being a complete loss of awareness of present surroundings.) Such trauma specific reenactment may occur in play.

1. Intense or prolonged psychological distress at exposure to internal or external cues that symbolize or resemble an aspect of the traumatic event(s).
2. Marked physiological reactions to reminders of the traumatic event(s).
3. One (or more) of the following symptoms, representing either persistent avoidance of stimuli associated with the traumatic event(s) or negative alterations in cognitions and mood associated with the traumatic event(s), must be present, beginning after the vent(s) or worsening after the event(s):

Persistent Avoidance of Stimuli

- Avoidance of or efforts to avoid activities, places, or physical reminders that arouse recollections of the traumatic event(s).

- Avoidance of or efforts to avoid people, conversations, or interpersonal situations that arouse recollections of the traumatic event(s).

Negative Alterations in Cognitions

- Substantially increased frequency of negative emotional states (e.g., fear, guilt, sadness, shame, confusion).
- Markedly diminished interest or participation in significant activities, including con- striction of play.
- Socially withdrawn behavior.
- Persistent reduction in expression of positive emotions.
  - Alterations in arousal and reactivity associated with the traumatic event(s), beginning, or worsening after the traumatic event(s) occurred, as evidenced by two (or more) of the following:
- Irritable behavior and angry outbursts (with little or no provocation) typically expressed as verbal or physical aggression toward people or objects (including extreme temper tantrums).
- Hypervigilance.
- Exaggerated startle response.
- Problems with concentration.
- Sleep disturbance (e.g., difficulty falling or staying asleep or restless sleep).

- The duration of the disturbance is more than 1 month.

- The disturbance causes clinically significant distress or impairment in relationships with parents, siblings, peers, or other caregivers or with school behavior.

- The disturbance is not attributable to the physiological effects of a substance (e.g., medication or alcohol) or another medical condition.

Specify whether:
With dissociative symptoms: The individual's symptoms meet the criteria for post-traumatic stress disorder, and the individual experiences persistent or recurrent symptoms of either of the following:

- Depersonalization: Persistent or recurrent experiences of feeling detached from, and as if one were an outside observer of, one's mental processes or body (e.g., feeling as though one were in a dream; feeling a sense of unreality of self or body or of time moving slowly).

- Derealization: Persistent or recurrent experiences of unreality of surroundings (e.g., the world around the individual is experienced as unreal, dreamlike, distant, or distorted).

Note: To use this subtype, the dissociative symptoms must not be attributable to the physiological effects of a substance (e.g., blackouts) or another medical condition (e.g., complex partial seizures).

Specify if:
With delayed expression: If the full diagnostic criteria are not met until at least 6 months after the event (although the onset and expression of some symptoms may be immediate).

Diagnostic Features

The essential feature of posttraumatic stress disorder (PTSD) is the development of characteristic symptoms following exposure to one or more traumatic events. Emotional reactions to the traumatic event (e.g., fear, helplessness, horror) are no longer a part of Criterion A.

The clinical presentation of PTSD varies. In some individuals, fear based reexperiencing, emotional, and behavioral symptoms may predominate. In others, anhedonic or dysphoric mood states and negative cognitions may be most distressing. In some other individuals, arousal and reactive-externalizing symptoms are prominent, while in others, dissociative symptoms predominate. Finally, some individuals exhibit combinations of these symptom patterns.

The directly experienced traumatic events in Criterion A include, but are not limited to, exposure to war as a combatant or civilian, threatened or actual physical assault (e.g., physical attack, robbery, mugging, childhood physical abuse), threatened or actual sexual violence (e.g., forced sexual penetration, alcohol/drug facilitated sexual penetration, abusive sexual contact, noncontact sexual abuse, sexual trafficking), being kidnapped, being taken hostage, terrorist attack, torture, incarceration as a prisoner of war, natural or human-made disasters, and severe motor vehicle accidents.

For children, sexually violent events may include developmentally inappropriate sexual experiences without physical violence or injury. A life-threatening illness or debilitating medical condition is not necessarily considered a traumatic event.

Medical incidents that qualify as traumatic events involve sudden, catastrophic events (e.g., waking during surgery, anaphylactic shock). Witnessed events include, but are not limited to, observing threatened or serious injury, unnatural death, physical or sexual abuse of another person due to violent assault, domestic violence, accident, war or disaster, or a medical catastrophe in one's child (e.g., a life-threatening hemorrhage). Indirect exposure through learning about an event is limited to experiences affecting close relatives or friends and experiences that are violent or accidental (e.g., death due to natural causes does not qualify). Such events include violent personal assault, suicide, serious accident, and serious injury. The disorder may be especially severe or long-lasting when the stressor is interpersonal and intentional (e.g., torture, sexual violence).

The traumatic event can be reexperienced in various ways. Commonly, the individual has recurrent, involuntary, and intrusive recollections of the event (Criterion B1). Intrusive recollections in PTSD are distinguished from depressive rumination in that they apply only to involuntary and intrusive distressing memories. The emphasis is on recurrent memories of the event that usually include sensory, emotional, or physiological behavioral components. A common reexperiencing symptom is distressing dreams that replay the event itself or that are representative or thematically related to the major threats involved in the traumatic event (Criterion B2). The individual may experience dissociative states that last from a few seconds to several hours or even days, during which components of the event are relived and the individual behaves as if the event were occurring at that moment (Criterion B3). Such events occur on a continuum from brief visual or other sensory intrusions about part of the traumatic event without loss of reality orientation, to complete loss of awareness of present surroundings. These episodes, often referred to as "flash- backs," are typically brief but can be associated with prolonged distress and heightened arousal. For young children, reenactment of events related to trauma may appear in play or in dissociative states. Intense psychological distress (Criterion B4) or physiological re-activity (Criterion B5) often occurs when the individual is exposed to triggering events that resemble or symbolize an aspect of the traumatic event (e.g., windy days after a hurricane; seeing someone who resembles one's perpetrator). The triggering cue could be a physical sensation (e.g., dizziness for survivors of head trauma; rapid heartbeat for a previously traumatized child), particularly for individuals with highly somatic presentations.

Stimuli associated with the trauma are persistently (e.g., always, or almost always) avoided. The individual commonly makes deliberate efforts to avoid thoughts, memories, feelings, or talking about the traumatic event (e.g., utilizing distraction techniques to avoid internal reminders) (Criterion C1) and to avoid activities, objects, situations, or people who arouse recollections of it (Criterion C2).

Negative alterations in cognitions or mood associated with the event begin or worsen after exposure to the event. These negative alterations can take various forms, including an inability to remember an important aspect of the traumatic event; such amnesia is typically due to dissociative amnesia and is not due

to head injury, alcohol, or drugs (Criterion D1). Another form is persistent (i.e., always, or almost always) and exaggerated negative expectations regarding important aspects of life applied to oneself, others, or the future (e.g., "I have always had bad judgment"; "People in authority can't be trusted")
that may manifest as a negative change in perceived identity since the trauma (e.g., "I can't trust anyone ever again"; Criterion D2).
Individuals with PTSD may have persistent erroneous cognitions about the causes of the traumatic event that lead them to blame themselves or others (e.g., "It's all my fault that my uncle abused me") (Criterion D3). A persistent negative mood state (e.g., fear, horror, anger, guilt, shame) either began or worsened after exposure to the event (Criterion D4). The individual may experience markedly diminished interest or participation in previously enjoyed activities (Criterion D5), feeling detached or estranged from other people (Criterion D6), or a persistent inability to feel positive emotions (especially happiness, joy, satisfaction, or emotions associated with intimacy, tenderness, and sexuality) (Criterion D7). Individuals with PTSD may be quick tempered and may even engage in aggressive verbal and/or physical behavior with little or no provocation (e.g., yelling at people, getting into fights, destroying objects) (Criterion E1).
They may also engage in reckless or self-destructive behavior such as dangerous driving, excessive alcohol, or drug use, or self- injurious or suicidal behavior (Criterion E2). PTSD is often characterized by a heightened sensitivity to potential threats, including those that are related to the traumatic experience (e.g., following a motor vehicle accident, being especially sensitive to the threat potentially caused by cars or trucks) and those not related to the traumatic event (e.g., being fearful of suffering a heart attack) (Criterion E3). Individuals with PTSD may be very reactive to unexpected stimuli, displaying a heightened startle response, or jumpiness, to loud noises or unexpected movements (e.g., jumping markedly in response to a telephone ringing) (Criterion E4).
Concentration difficulties, including difficulty remembering daily events (e.g., forgetting one's telephone number) or attending to focused tasks (e.g., following a conversation for a sustained period of time), are commonly reported (Criterion E5).
Problems with sleep onset and maintenance are common and may be associated with nightmares and safety concerns or with generalized elevated arousal that

interferes with adequate sleep (Criterion E6). Some individuals also experience persistent dissociative symptoms of detachment from their bodies (depersonalization) or the world around them (derealization); this is reflected in the "with dissociative symptoms" specifier.

Associated Features Supporting Diagnosis

Developmental regression, such as loss of language in young children, may occur. Auditory pseudo-hallucinations, such as having the sensory experience of hearing one's thoughts spoken in one or more different voices, as well as paranoid ideation, can be present. Following prolonged, repeated, and severe traumatic events (e.g., childhood abuse, torture), the individual may additionally experience difficulties in regulating emotions or maintaining stable interpersonal relationships, or dissociative symptoms. When the traumatic event produces violent death, symptoms of both problematic bereavement and PTSD may be present.

Prevalence

In the United States, projected lifetime risk for PTSD using DSM-IV criteria at age 75 years is 8.7%. Twelve-month prevalence among U.S. adults is about 3.5%. Lower estimates are seen in Europe and most Asian, African, and Latin American countries, clustering around 0.5%. Although different groups have different levels of exposure to traumatic events, the conditional probability of developing PTSD following a similar level of exposure may also vary across cultural groups.

Rates of PTSD are higher among veterans and others whose vocation increases the risk of traumatic exposure (e.g., police, firefighters, emergency medical personnel). Highest rates (ranging from one-third to more than one- half of those exposed) are found among survivors of rape, military combat, and captivity, and ethnically or politically motivated internment and genocide. The prevalence of PTSD may vary across development; children and adolescents, including preschool children, generally have displayed lower prevalence following exposure to serious traumatic events; however, this may be because previous criteria were insufficiently developmentally informed. The prevalence of full-threshold PTSD also appears to be lower among older adults compared with the general population; there is evidence that subthreshold presentations are more common than full PTSD in later life and that these symptoms are associated with substantial clinical impairment. Compared with U.S.

non-Latino whites, higher rates of PTSD have been reported among U.S. Latinos, African Americans, and American Indians, and lower rates have been reported among Asian Americans, after adjustment for traumatic exposure and demographic variables.

Development and Course

PTSD can occur at any age, beginning after the first year of life. Symptoms usually begin within the first 3 months after the trauma, although there may be a delay of months, or even years, before criteria for the diagnosis are met. There is abundant evidence for what DSMIV called "delayed onset" but is now called "delayed expression," with the recognition that some symptoms typically appear immediately and that the delay is in meeting full criteria.

Frequently, an individual's reaction to a trauma initially meets criteria for acute stress disorder in the immediate aftermath of the trauma. The symptoms of PTSD and the relative predominance of different symptoms may vary over time. Duration of the symptoms also varies, with complete recovery within 3 months occurring in approximately one-half of adults, while some individuals remain symptomatic for longer than 12 months and sometimes for more than 50 years. Symptom recurrence and intensification may occur in response to reminders of the original trauma, ongoing life stressors, or newly experienced traumatic events. For older individuals, declining health, worsening cognitive functioning, and social isolation may exacerbate PTSD symptoms.

The clinical expression of reexperiencing can vary across development. Young children may report new onset of frightening dreams without content specific to the traumatic event. Before age 6 years (see criteria for preschool subtype), young children are more likely to express reexperiencing symptoms through play that refers directly or symbolically to the trauma. They may not manifest fearful reactions at the time of the exposure or during reexperiencing. Parents may report a wide range of emotional or behavioral changes in young children. Children may focus on imagined interventions in their play or storytelling. In addition to avoidance, children may become preoccupied with reminders. Because of young children's limitations in expressing thoughts or labeling emotions, negative alterations in mood or cognition tend to involve primarily mood changes. Children may experience co- occurring traumas (e.g., physical abuse, witnessing domestic violence) and in chronic circumstances may not be able to identify onset of symptomatology.

Avoidant behavior may be associated with restricted play or exploratory behavior in young children; reduced participation in new activities in school-age children; or reluctance to pursue developmental opportunities in adolescents (e.g., dating, driving). Older children and adolescents may judge themselves as cowardly. Adolescents may harbor beliefs of being changed in ways that make them socially undesirable and estrange them from peers (e.g., "Now I'll never fit in") and lose aspirations for the future. Irritable or aggressive behavior in children and adolescents can interfere with peer relationships and school behavior. Reckless behavior may lead to accidental injury to self or others, thrill-seeking, or high-risk behaviors. Individuals who continue to experience PTSD into older adulthood may express fewer symptoms of hyperarousal, avoidance, and negative cognitions and mood compared with younger adults with PTSD, although adults exposed to traumatic events during later life may display more avoidance, hyperarousal, sleep problems, and crying spells than do younger adults exposed to the same traumatic events. In older individuals, the disorder is associated with negative health perceptions, primary care utilization, and suicidal ideation.

Risk and Prognostic Factors

Risk (and protective) factors are generally divided into pre-traumatic, peritraumatic, and posttraumatic factors.

Pretraumatic factors

Temperamental. These include childhood emotional problems by age 6 years (e.g., prior traumatic exposure, externalizing or anxiety problems) and prior mental disorders (e.g., panic disorder, depressive disorder, PTSD, or obsessive-compulsive disorder (OCD).

Environmental. These include lower socioeconomic status; lower education; exposure to prior trauma (especially during childhood); childhood adversity (e.g., economic deprivation, family dysfunction, parental separation, or death); cultural characteristics (e.g., fatalistic, or self-blaming coping strategies); lower intelligence; minority racial/ethnic status; and a family psychiatric history. Social support prior to event exposure is protective.

Genetic and physiological. These include female gender and younger age at the time of trauma exposure (for adults). Certain genotypes may either be protective or increase risk of PTSD after exposure to traumatic events.

Peritraumatic factors

Environmental. These include severity (dose) of the trauma (the greater the magnitude of trauma, the greater the likelihood of PTSD), perceived life threat, personal injury, interpersonal violence (particularly trauma perpetrated by a caregiver or involving a witnessed threat to a caregiver in children), and, for military personnel, being a perpetrator, witnessing atrocities, or killing the enemy. Finally, dissociation that occurs during the trauma and persists afterward is a risk factor.

Posttraumatic factors Temperamental. These include negative appraisals, inappropriate coping strategies, and development of acute stress disorder.

Environmental. These include subsequent exposure to repeated upsetting reminders, subsequent adverse life events, and financial or other trauma-related losses. Social support (including family stability, for children) is a protective factor that moderates outcome after trauma.

Suicide Risk

Traumatic events such as childhood abuse increase a person's suicide risk. PTSD is associated with suicidal ideation and suicide attempts, and presence of the disorder may indicate which individuals with ideation eventually make a suicide plan or actually attempt suicide.

Functional Consequences of Posttraumatic Stress Disorder

PTSD is associated with high levels of social, occupational, and physical disability, as well as considerable economic costs and high levels of medical utilization. Impaired functioning is exhibited across social, interpersonal, developmental, educational, physical health, and occupational domains. In community and veteran samples, PTSD is associated with poor social and family relationships, absenteeism from work, lower income, and lower educational and occupational success.

Differential Diagnosis

Adjustment disorders. In adjustment disorders, the stressor can be of any severity or type rather than that required by PTSD Criterion A. The diagnosis of an adjustment disorder is used when the response to a stressor that meets PTSD Criterion A does not meet all other PTSD criteria (or criteria for another mental disorder). An adjustment disorder is also diagnosed when the symptom pattern of PTSD occurs in response to a stressor that does not meet PTSD Criterion A (e.g., spouse leaving, being fired).

Other posttraumatic disorders and conditions. Not all psychopathology that occurs in individuals exposed to an extreme stressor should necessarily be attributed to PTSD. The diagnosis requires that trauma exposure precede the onset or exacerbation of pertinent symptoms. Moreover, if the symptom response pattern to the extreme stressor meets criteria for another mental disorder, these diagnoses should be given instead of, or in addition to, PTSD. Other diagnoses and conditions are excluded if they are better explained by PTSD (e.g., symptoms of panic disorder that occur only after exposure to traumatic reminders). If severe, symptom response patterns to the extreme stressor may warrant a separate diagnosis (e.g., dissociative amnesia).

Acute stress disorder. Acute stress disorder is distinguished from PTSD because the symptom pattern in acute stress disorder is restricted to a duration of 3 days to 1 month following exposure to the traumatic event.

Anxiety disorders and obsessive-compulsive disorder. In OCD, there are recurrent intrusive thoughts, but these meet the definition of an obsession. In addition, the intrusive thoughts are not related to an experienced traumatic event, compulsions are usually present, and other symptoms of PTSD or acute stress disorder are typically absent. Neither the arousal and dissociative symptoms of panic disorder nor the avoidance, irritability, and anxiety of generalized anxiety disorder are associated with a specific traumatic event. The symptoms of separation anxiety disorder are clearly related to separation from home or family, rather than to a traumatic event.

Major depressive disorder. Major depression may or may not be preceded by a traumatic event and should be diagnosed if other PTSD symptoms are absent. Specifically, major depressive disorder does not include any PTSD Criterion B or C symptoms. Nor does it include a number of symptoms from PTSD Criterion D or E.

Personality disorders. Interpersonal difficulties that had their onset, or were greatly exacerbated, after exposure to a traumatic event may be an indication of PTSD, rather than a personality disorder, in which such difficulties would be expected independently of any traumatic exposure.

Dissociative disorders. Dissociative amnesia, dissociative identity disorder, and depersonalization-derealization disorder may or may not be preceded by exposure to a traumatic event or may or may not have co-occurring PTSD symptoms. When full PTSD criteria are also met, however, the PTSD "with dissociative symptoms" subtype should be considered.

Conversion disorder (functional neurological symptom disorder). New onset of somatic symptoms within the context of posttraumatic distress might be an indication of PTSD rather than conversion disorder (functional neurological symptom disorder).

Psychotic disorders. Flashbacks in PTSD must be distinguished from illusions, hallucinations, and other perceptual disturbances that may occur in schizophrenia, brief psychotic disorder, and other psychotic disorders; depressive and bipolar disorders with psychotic features; delirium; substance/medication-induced disorders; and psychotic disorders due to another medical condition.

Traumatic brain injury. When a brain injury occurs in the context of a traumatic event (e.g., traumatic accident, bomb blast, acceleration/deceleration trauma), symptoms of PTSD may appear.

An event causing head trauma may also constitute a psychological traumatic event, and traumatic brain injury (TBI)-related neurocognitive symptoms are not mutually exclusive and may occur concurrently. Symptoms previously termed postconcussive (e.g., headaches, dizziness, sensitivity to light or sound, irritability, concentration deficits) can occur in brain- injured and non-brain injured populations, including individuals with PTSD. Because symptoms of PTSD and TBI-related neurocognitive symptoms can overlap, a differential diagnosis between PTSD and neurocognitive disorder symptoms attributable to TBI may be possible based on the presence of symptoms that are distinctive to each presentation. Whereas re-experiencing and avoidance are characteristic of PTSD and not the effects of TBI, persistent disorientation and confusion are more specific to TBI (neurocognitive effects) than to PTSD.

Comorbidity

Individuals with PTSD are 80% more likely than those without PTSD to have symptoms that meet diagnostic criteria for at least one other mental disorder (e.g., depressive, bipolar, anxiety, or substance use disorders).

Comorbid substance use disorder and conduct disorder are more common among males than among females. Among U.S. military personnel and combat veterans who have been deployed to recent wars in Afghanistan and Iraq, co-occurrence of PTSD and mild TBI is 48%. Although most young children with PTSD also have at least one other diagnosis, the patterns of comorbidity are different than in adults, with oppositional defiant disorder and separation anxiety disorder predominating. Finally, there is considerable comorbidity between PTSD and major neurocognitive disorder and some overlapping symptoms between these disorders.

Acute Stress Disorder Diagnostic Criteria 308.3 (F43.0)

- Exposure to actual or threatened death, serious injury, or sexual violation in one (or more) of the following ways:

- Directly experiencing the traumatic event(s).

- Witnessing, in person, the event(s) as it occurred to others.

- Learning that the event(s) occurred to a close family member or close friend. Note: In cases of actual or threatened death of a family member or friend, the event(s) must have been violent or accidental.

- Experiencing repeated or extreme exposure to aversive details of the traumatic event(s) (e.g., first responders collecting human remains, police officers repeatedly exposed to details of child abuse).

Note: This does not apply to exposure through electronic media, television, movies, or pictures, unless this exposure is work related.

- Presence of nine (or more) of the following symptoms from any of the five categories of intrusion, negative mood, dissociation, avoidance, and arousal, beginning or worsening after the traumatic event(s) occurred:

Intrusion Symptoms

- Recurrent, involuntary, and intrusive distressing memories of the traumatic event(s). Note: In children, repetitive play may occur in which themes or aspects of the traumatic event(s) are expressed.

- Recurrent distressing dreams in which the content and/or effect of the dream are related to the event(s). Note: In children, there may be frightening dreams without recognizable content.

- Dissociative reactions (e.g., flashbacks) in which the individual feels or acts as if the traumatic event(s) were recurring. (Such reactions may occur on a continuum, with the most extreme expression being a complete loss of awareness of present surroundings.) Note: In children, trauma-specific reenactment may occur in play.

- Intense or prolonged psychological distress or marked physiological reactions in response to internal or external cues that symbolize or resemble an aspect of the traumatic event(s).

Negative Mood

- Persistent inability to experience positive emotions (e.g., inability to experience happiness, satisfaction, or loving feelings).

Dissociative Symptoms

- An altered sense of the reality of one's surroundings or oneself (e.g., seeing oneself from another's perspective, being in a daze, time slowing).

- Inability to remember an important aspect of the traumatic event(s) (typically due to dissociative amnesia and not to other factors such as head injury, alcohol, or drugs).

Avoidance Symptoms

- Efforts to avoid distressing memories, thoughts, or feelings about or closely associated with the traumatic event(s).

- Efforts to avoid external reminders (people, places, conversations, activities, objects, situations) that arouse distressing memories, thoughts, or feelings about or closely associated with the traumatic event(s).

Arousal Symptoms

• Sleep disturbance (e.g., difficulty falling or staying asleep, restless sleep).

• Irritable behavior and angry outbursts (with little or no provocation), typically ex- pressed as verbal or physical aggression toward people or objects.

• Hypervigilance.

• Problems with concentration.

• Exaggerated startle response.

• Duration of the disturbance (symptoms in Criterion B) is 3 days to 1 month after trauma exposure.

Note: Symptoms typically begin immediately after the trauma, but persistence for at least 3 days and up to a month is needed to meet disorder criteria.

• The disturbance causes clinically significant distress or impairment in social, occupational, or other important areas of functioning.

• The disturbance is not attributable to the physiological effects of a substance (e.g., medication or alcohol) or another medical condition (e.g., mild traumatic brain injury) and is not better explained by brief psychotic disorder.

Diagnostic Features

The essential feature of acute stress disorder is the development of characteristic symptoms lasting from 3 days to 1 month following exposure to one or more traumatic events. Traumatic events that are experienced directly include, but are not limited to, exposure to war as a combatant or civilian, threatened or actual violent personal assault (e.g., sexual violence, physical attack, active combat, mugging, childhood physical and/or sexual violence, being kidnapped, being taken hostage, terrorist attack, torture), natural or human- made disasters (e.g., earthquake, hurricane, airplane crash), and severe accident (e.g., severe motor vehicle, industrial accident). For children, sexually traumatic events may include inappropriate sexual experiences without violence or injury. A life-threatening illness or debilitating medical condition is not necessarily considered a traumatic event. Medical incidents that qualify as traumatic events involve sudden, catastrophic events (e.g., waking during surgery, anaphylactic shock). Stressful events that do not possess the severe and traumatic components of events encompassed by Criterion A may lead to an adjustment disorder but not to acute stress disorder.

The clinical presentation of acute stress disorder may vary by individual but typically involves an anxiety response that includes some form of reexperiencing of or reactivity to the traumatic event. In some individuals, a dissociative or detached presentation can predominate, although these individuals typically will also display strong emotional or physiological reactivity in response to trauma reminders. In other individuals, there can be a strong anger response in which reactivity is characterized by irritable or possibly aggressive responses. The full symptom picture must be present for at least 3 days after the traumatic event and can be diagnosed only up to 1 month after the event. Symptoms that occur immediately after the event but resolve in less than 3 days would not meet criteria for acute stress disorder.

Witnessed events include, but are not limited to, observing threatened or serious injury, unnatural death, physical or sexual violence inflicted on another individual as a result of violent assault, severe domestic violence, severe accident, war, and disaster; it may also include witnessing a medical catastrophe (e.g., a life-threatening hemorrhage) involving one's child. Events experienced indirectly through learning about the event are limited to close relatives or close friends. Such events must have been violent or accidental death due to natural causes does not qualify and include violent personal assault, suicide, serious accident, or serious injury. The disorder may be especially severe when the stressor is interpersonal and intentional (e.g., torture, rape). The likelihood of developing this disorder may increase as the intensity of and physical proximity to the stressor increase.

The traumatic event can be reexperienced in various ways. Commonly, the individual has recurrent and intrusive recollections of the event (Criterion Bl). The recollections are spontaneous or triggered recurrent memories of the event that usually occur in response to a stimulus that is reminiscent of the traumatic experience (e.g., the sound of a backfiring car triggering memories of gunshots). These intrusive memories often include sensory (e.g., sensing the intense heat that was perceived in a house fire), emotional (e.g., experiencing the fear of believing that one was about to be stabbed), or physiological (e.g., experiencing the shortness of breath that one suffered during a near-drowning) components. Distressing dreams may contain themes that are representative of or thematically related to the major threats involved in the traumatic event. (For example, in the case of a motor vehicle accident survivor, the distressing dreams may involve crashing cars generally; in the case of a combat soldier, the distressing dreams may involve being harmed in ways other than combat.)

Dissociative states may last from a few seconds to several hours, or even days, during which components of the event are relived and the individual behaves as though experiencing the event at that moment. While dissociative responses are common during a traumatic event, only dissociative responses that persist beyond 3 days after trauma exposure are considered for the diagnosis of acute stress disorder. For young children, reenactment of events related to trauma may appear in play and may include dissociative moments (e.g., a child who survives a motor vehicle accident may repeatedly crash toy cars during play in a focused and distressing manner). These episodes, often referred to as flashbacks, are typically brief but involve a sense that the traumatic event is occurring in the present rather than being remembered in the past and are associated with significant distress.

Some individuals with the disorder do not have intrusive memories of the event itself, but instead experience intense psychological distress or physiological reactivity when they are exposed to triggering events that resemble or symbolize an aspect of the traumatic event (e.g., windy days for children after a hurricane, entering an elevator for a male or female who was raped in an elevator, seeing someone who resembles one's perpetrator). The triggering cue could be a physical sensation (e.g., a sense of heat for a bum victim, dizziness for survivors of head trauma), particularly for individuals with highly somatic presentations. The individual may have a persistent inability to feel positive emotions (e.g., happiness, joy, satisfaction, or emotions associated with intimacy, tenderness, or sexuality) but can experience negative emotions such as fear, sadness, anger, guilt, or shame.

Alterations in awareness can include depersonalization, a detached sense of oneself (e.g., seeing oneself from the other side of the room), or derealization, having a distorted view of one's surroundings (e.g., perceiving things are moving in slow motion, seeing things in a daze, not being aware of events that one would normally encode). Some individuals also report an inability to remember an important aspect of the traumatic event that was presumably encoded. This symptom is attributable to dissociative amnesia and is not attributable to head injury, alcohol, or drugs. Stimuli associated with the trauma

are persistently avoided. The individual may refuse to discuss the traumatic experience or may engage in avoidance strategies to minimize awareness of emotional reactions (e.g., excessive alcohol use when reminded of the experience). This behavioral avoidance may include avoiding watching news coverage of the traumatic experience, refusing to return to a workplace where the trauma occurred, or avoiding interacting with others who shared the same traumatic experience.

It is very common for individuals with acute stress disorder to experience problems with sleep onset and maintenance, which may be associated with nightmares or with generalized elevated arousal that prevents adequate sleep. Individuals with acute stress dis- order may be quick tempered and may even engage in aggressive verbal and/or physical behavior with little provocation. Acute stress disorder is often characterized by a heightened sensitivity to potential threats, including those that are related to the traumatic experience (e.g., a motor vehicle accident victim may be especially sensitive to the threat potentially caused by any cars or trucks) or those not related to the traumatic event (e.g., fear of having a heart attack). Concentration difficulties, including difficulty remembering daily events (e.g., forgetting one's telephone number) or attending to focused tasks (e.g., following a conversation for a sustained period of time), are commonly reported.

Individuals with acute stress disorder may be very reactive to unexpected stimuli, displaying a heightened startle response or jumpiness to loud noises or unexpected movements (e.g., the individual may jump markedly in the response to a telephone ringing).

Associated Features Supporting Diagnosis

Individuals with acute stress disorder commonly engage in catastrophic or extremely negative thoughts about their role in the traumatic event, their response to the traumatic experience, or the likelihood of future harm. For example, an individual with acute stress disorder may feel excessively guilty about not having prevented the traumatic event or about not adapting to the experience more successfully. Individuals with acute stress disorder may also interpret their symptoms in a catastrophic manner, such that flashback memories or emotional numbing may be interpreted as a sign of diminished mental capacity. It is common for individuals with acute stress disorder to experience panic attacks in the initial month after trauma exposure that may be triggered by trauma reminders or may apparently occur spontaneously.

Additionally, individuals with acute stress disorder may display chaotic or impulsive behavior. For example, individuals may drive recklessly, make irrational decisions, or gamble excessively. In children, there may be significant separation anxiety, possibly manifested by excessive needs for attention from caregivers.

In the case of bereavement following a death that occurred in traumatic circumstances, the symptoms of acute stress disorder can involve acute grief reactions. In such cases, reexperiencing, dissociative, and arousal symptoms may involve reactions to the loss, such as intrusive memories of the circumstances of the individual's death, disbelief that the individual has died, and anger about the death. Postconcussive symptoms (e.g., headaches, dizziness, sensitivity to light or sound, irritability, concentration deficits), which occur frequently following mild traumatic brain injury, are also frequently seen in individuals with acute stress disorder. Postconcussive symptoms are equally common in brain-injured and non-brain-injured populations, and the frequent occurrence of postconcussive symptoms could be attributable to acute stress disorder symptoms.

Prevalence

The prevalence of acute stress disorder in recently trauma-exposed populations (i.e., within 1 month of trauma exposure) varies according to the nature of the event and the context in which it is assessed. In both U.S. and non-U.S.

populations, acute stress disorder tends to be identified in less than 20% of cases following traumatic events that do not in- volve interpersonal assault; 13%-21% of motor vehicle accidents, 14% of mild traumatic brain injury, 19% of assault, 10% of severe burns, and 6%-12% of industrial accidents. Higher rates (i.e., 20%-50%) are reported following interpersonal traumatic events, including assault, rape, and witnessing a mass shooting.

Development and Course

Acute stress disorder cannot be diagnosed until 3 days after a traumatic event. Although acute stress disorder may progress to posttraumatic stress disorder (PTSD) after 1 month, it may also be a transient stress response that remits within 1 month of trauma exposure and does not result in PTSD. Approximately half of individuals who eventually develop PTSD initially present with acute stress disorder. Symptom worsening during the initial month can occur, often as a result of ongoing life stressors or further traumatic events.

The forms of reexperiencing can vary across development. Unlike adults or adolescents, young children may report frightening dreams without content that clearly reflects aspects of the trauma (e.g., waking in fright in the aftermath of the trauma but being unable to relate the content of the dream to the traumatic event). Children aged 6 years and younger are more likely than older children to express reexperiencing symptoms through play that refers directly or symbolically to the trauma. For example, a very young child who survived a fire may draw pictures of flames. Young children also do not necessarily manifest fearful reactions at the time of the exposure or even during reexperiencing. Parents typically report a range of emotional expressions, such as anger, shame, or withdrawal, and even excessively bright positive affect, in young children who are traumatized. Although children may avoid reminders of the trauma, they sometimes become preoccupied with reminders (e.g., a young child bitten by a dog may talk about dogs constantly yet avoid going outside because of fear of coming into contact with a dog).

Adjustment Disorders Diagnostic Criteria

1. The development of emotional or behavioral symptoms in response to an identifiable stressor(s) occurring within 3 months of the onset of the stressor(s).

2. These symptoms or behaviors are clinically significant, as evidenced by one or both of the following:

1. Marked distress that is out of proportion to the severity or intensity of the stressor, taking into account the external context and the cultural factors that might influence symptom severity and presentation.
2. Significant impairment in social, occupational, or other important areas of functioning.
3. The stress-related disturbance does not meet the criteria for another mental disorder and is not merely an exacerbation of a preexisting mental disorder.
4. The symptoms do not represent normal bereavement.
5. Once the stressor or its consequences have terminated, the symptoms do not persist for more than an additional 6 months. Specify whether:
6. 309.0 (F43.21) With depressed mood: Low mood, tearfulness, or feelings of hopelessness are predominant.

309.24 (F43.22) With anxiety: Nervousness, worry, jitteriness, or separation anxiety is predominant.

309.28 (F43.23) With mixed anxiety and depressed mood: A combination of de- pression and anxiety is predominant.

309.3 (F43.24) With disturbance of conduct: Disturbance of conduct is predominant.

309.4 (F43.25) With mixed disturbance of emotions and conduct: Both emotional symptoms (e.g., depression, anxiety) and a disturbance of conduct are predominant.

309.9 (F43.20) Unspecified: For maladaptive reactions that are not classifiable as one of the specific subtypes of adjustment disorder.

Diagnostic Features

The presence of emotional or behavioral symptoms in response to an identifiable stressor is the essential feature of adjustment disorders: (Criterion A). The stressor may be a single event (e.g., a termination of a romantic relationship), or there may be multiple stressors (e.g., marked business difficulties and marital problems). Stressors may be recurrent (e.g., associated with seasonal business crises, unfulfilling sexual relationships) or continuous (e.g., a persistent painful illness with increasing disability, living in a crime-ridden neighborhood).

Stressors may affect a single individual, an entire family, or a larger group or community (e.g., a natural disaster). Some stressors may accompany specific developmental events (e.g., going to school, leaving a parental home, reentering a parental home, getting married, becoming a parent, failing to attain occupational goals, retirement).

Adjustment disorders may be diagnosed following the death of a loved one when the intensity, quality, or persistence of grief reactions exceeds what normally might be expected, when cultural, religious, or age-appropriate norms are taken into account. A more specific set of bereavement-related symptoms has been designated persistent complex bereavement disorder.

Adjustment disorders are associated with an increased risk of suicide attempts and completed suicide.

Prevalence

Adjustment disorders are common, although prevalence may vary widely as a function of the population studied and the assessment methods used. The percentage of individuals in outpatient mental health treatment with a principal diagnosis of an adjustment disorder ranges from approximately 5% to 20%. In a hospital psychiatric consultation setting, it is often the most common diagnosis, frequently reaching 50%.

Development and Course

By definition, the disturbance in adjustment disorders begins within 3 months of onset of a stressor and lasts no longer than 6 months after the stressor or its consequences have ceased. If the stressor is an acute event (e.g., being fired from a job), the onset of the disturbance is usually immediate (i.e., within a few days) and the duration is relatively brief (i.e., no more than a few months). If the stressor or its consequences persist, the adjustment disorder may also continue to be present and become the persistent form.

Risk and Prognostic Factors

Environmental: Individuals from disadvantaged life circumstances experience a high rate of stressors and may be at increased risk for adjustment disorders.

Culture-Related Diagnostic issues

The context of the individual's cultural setting should be taken into account in making the clinical judgment of whether the individual's response to the stressor is maladaptive or whether the associated distress is in excess of what would be expected. The nature, meaning, and experience of the stressors and the evaluation of the response to the stressors may vary across cultures.

Functional Consequences of Adjustment Disorders

The subjective distress or impairment in functioning associated with adjustment disorders is frequently manifested as decreased performance at work or school and temporary changes in social relationships. An adjustment disorder may complicate the course of illness in individuals who have a general medical condition (e.g., decreased compliance with the recommended medical regimen; increased length of hospital stay).

Differential Diagnosis

Major depressive disorder. If an individual has symptoms that meet criteria for a major depressive disorder in response to a stressor, the diagnosis of an adjustment disorder is not applicable. The symptom profile of major depressive disorder differentiates it from adjustment disorders.

Posttraumatic stress disorder and acute stress disorder. In adjustment disorders, the stressor can be of any severity rather than of the severity and type required by Criterion A of acute stress disorder and posttraumatic stress disorder (PTSD). In distinguishing adjustment disorders from these two posttraumatic diagnoses, there are both timing and symptom profile considerations. Adjustment disorders can be diagnosed immediately and persist up to 6 months after exposure to the traumatic event, whereas acute stress disorder can only occur between 3 days and 1 month of exposure to the stressor, and PTSD cannot be diagnosed until at least 1 month has passed since the occurrence of the traumatic stressor. The required symptom profile for PTSD and acute stress disorder differentiates them from the adjustment disorders. With regard to symptom profiles, an adjustment disorder may be diagnosed following a traumatic event when an individual exhibits symptom of either acute stress disorder or PTSD that do not meet or exceed the diagnostic threshold for either disorder. An adjustment disorder should also be diagnosed for individuals who have not been exposed to a traumatic event but who otherwise exhibit the full symptom profile of either acute stress disorder or PTSD.

Personality disorders. With regard to personality disorders, some personality features may be associated with a vulnerability to situational distress that may resemble an adjustment disorder. The lifetime history of personality functioning will help inform the interpretation of distressed behaviors to aid in distinguishing a longstanding personality disorder from an adjustment disorder. In addition to some personality disorders incurring vulnerability to distress, stressors may also exacerbate personality disorder symptoms. In the presence of a personality disorder, if the symptom criteria for an adjustment disorder are met, and the stress-related disturbance exceeds what may be attributable to maladaptive personality disorder symptoms (i.e., Criterion C is met), then the diagnosis of an adjustment disorder should be made.

Psychological factors affecting other medical conditions. In psychological factors affecting other medical conditions, specific psychological entities (e.g., psychological symptoms, behaviors, other factors) exacerbate a medical condition. These psychological factors can precipitate, exacerbate, or put an individual at risk for medical illness, or they can worsen an existing condition. In contrast, an adjustment disorder is a reaction to the stressor (e.g., having a medical illness).

Normative stress reactions. When bad things happen, most people get upset. This is not an adjustment disorder. The diagnosis should only be made when the magnitude of the distress (e.g., alterations in mood, anxiety, or conduct) exceeds what would normally be expected (which may vary in different cultures) or when the adverse event precipitates functional impairment.

Comorbidity

Adjustment disorders can accompany most mental disorders and any medical disorder. Adjustment disorders can be diagnosed in addition to another mental disorder only if the latter does not explain the particular symptoms that occur in reaction to the stressor. For example, an individual may develop an adjustment disorder, with depressed mood, after losing a job and at the same time have a diagnosis of obsessive-compulsive disorder. Or an individual may have a depressive or bipolar disorder and an adjustment disorder as long as the criteria for both are met. Adjustment disorders are common accompaniments of medical illness and may be the major psychological response to a medical disorder.

Treatments and Medications Forms of Treatments

Psychotherapy

Psychotherapy is referred to as talk therapy. There are several types of psychotherapy. The success depends on the individual, the disorder, and the severity of the disorder.

Psychodynamic Psychotherapy

Psychodynamic psychotherapy goal is to assist people understand their problems and make changes. The technique is called insight-oriented psychotherapy and uses free association. People have a face-to-face session with the therapist and are encouraged to say thoughts that enter their mind, to find and understand unconscious conflicts stemming from childhood that have progressed into adulthood. Those most likely to benefit are people with certain personality disorders and chronic mental disorders such as anxiety disorder.

Interpersonal Therapy

Interpersonal therapy aims to enhance relationships and social interactions. This is accomplished by reassurance and support, clarification of feelings, and improving interpersonal communications. This type of therapy is used for those with major depression.

Supportive Psychotherapy

Supportive psychotherapy, the most common psychotherapy, seeks to maintain or restore a person's highest level of function. People dealing with highly stressful situations, severe medical issues, and mental disorders not responsive to other forms of therapy.

Cognitive-Behavior Therapy

Cognitive-Behavior therapy (CBT) is used to identify and change distortions in thinking and behaviors. Techniques used allows for identifying beliefs and attitudes, recognizing negative thought patterns and unhelpful behaviors; education in other ways of thinking.

Cognitive rehearsing (reviewing in the person's mind how to respond differently than in the past); homework assignments. This is used for those with major depressive disorder, anxiety disorder, substance abuse, and trauma-related disorders.

Dialectical Behavior Therapy
Dialectical Behavior therapy (DBT) is another form of CBT. DBT can be one-on-one or in a group session. DBT is helpful in the treatment of borderline personality disorder, severe depression, posttraumatic stress disorder, eating disorders, substance use disorders, and traumatic brain injury.

Behavioral Therapy
Behavioral therapy's goal is to replace unhealthy patterns of behavior with healthier ways to handle stress, fear, or worry. Behavior therapy works best for people who want to make changes, have anxiety disorders such as phobias, panic attacks, substance use disorders, and/or eating disorders.

The basic methods of behavior therapy are:

- Behavior modification: focusing on negative habits or behavior.

- Systemic desensitization: teaches how to reduce or control fear triggered by certain stimuli such as animals or settings such as going out in public.

- Relaxation training: helps to control mental and physical state.

- Exposure therapy: gradual stages of direct exposure to a feared object or situation to control anxiety without the use of relaxation technique. Exposure and response prevention therapy is helpful for obsessive-compulsive disorder. It can teach them for instance, to stop washing their hands so much after being exposed to a feared object.

- Flooding: exposes people to what they fear most and keeps them exposed with the assistance of the therapist until the fear lessens.

- Modeling: therapist performs a desired behavior that the person can copy.

- Assertiveness training: teaches how to express feelings and thoughts honestly and directly.

Couples, Martial, and Family Therapy

Couples, martial, and family therapy aims to change relationships, improve communications and interactions, and teach acceptable ways to resolve conflicts. The focus is on interaction between the group instead, the individual person's way of thinking.

Common types of family therapy are:

Behavioral family therapy: views problems and behaviors because of family attention and rewards, which support the behavior.

Structural family therapy: places value of family structure for helping the family function as whole as well as the impact on the well-being of the family members.

Group Therapy

Group therapy seeks to change ways of relating to others relieves distressing psychological symptoms. It gives people social interactions with others with the same disorder, it allows the therapist to help multiple people at the same time.

The basic approach is supportive, with use of cognitive behavior therapy, psychodynamic therapy, interpersonal or psychoanalytic therapy. It can provide self-disclosure and catharsis, sharing insight and gaining feedback from peers and therapist. Group therapy works best for those with similar mental and physical disorders for example, an eating disorder and PTSD; teens; psychiatric patients in hospital setting; and families with mental disorders.

Medications

Sometimes medication is needed to treat the symptoms. The following is a list of the types of medications used.

Antidepressants: SSRI which are serotonin reuptake inhibitors, SNRI serotonin-norepinephrine reuptake inhibitors, tricyclic antidepressants, tetracyclic antidepressants, and MAO monoamine oxidase inhibitors. They can be effective in treating, panic disorder, PTSD, generalized anxiety disorder, social phobia, OCD, borderline- personality disorder.

Antipsychotic Medications: used to treat psychotic symptoms such as hallucinations and delusions. They are used in the treatment of schizophrenia and other psychosis. They are used for manic and depressive episodes in bipolar disorder.

Sedatives, Hypnotics, and Anxiolytics: sedatives or anxiolytics are used to treat anxiety and insomnia. Hypnotics are used to cause and maintain sleep. Anxiolytics can be used to treat panic disorder until antidepression medication starts to work. Benzodiazepines is one class of anxiolytics. They have muscle relaxant and anticonvulsant feature (which helps to control seizures). Buspirone is another anxiolytic and is prescribed for generalized anxiety disorder. It is not useful for panic disorder.

Mood Stabilizers: help reduce mood swings and used in bipolar disorder. Mood stabilizer medications include lithium, valproate, carbamazepine, lamotrigine, and antipsychotic medications.

Stimulants: are usually prescribed for ADHD.

Other treatments: Electroconvulsive therapy and Transcranial magnetic therapy would be the last resort, if therapy, medication, or a combination of therapy and medication does not work. Living a healthy lifestyle can minimize symptoms.

Electroconvulsive Therapy: ECT is the passage of a controlled electrical current through the brain to induce a brief seizure. ECT is the best treatment for severe mental disorders. 80%-85% of those with severe depression improves.

Transcranial Magnetic Stimulation: TMS is a new form of treatment for depression. The treatment uses a device that creates an electronic pulse sent to certain areas of the brain. With TMS, a seizure is not induced.

Exercise and healthy eating: therapy takes time and commitment. People may not see improvement right away. One way people can help to feel better is by exercising. Does not have to be heavy lifting, just 20 minutes a day doing sone physical activity. Studies show that regular exercise can improve your mood. Eating healthy can combat physical ailments such as diabetes which makes it harder to focus on the mental aspect if the focus is on treating a chronic disease. If the person already has a chronic physical disease, eating healthier could improve the symptoms.

What is Parapsychology?

Parapsychology is considered a controversial science. The thought of investigating paranormal activities is difficult to fathom for the scientific community. In science, a problem or need is identified, then hypothesized, experiments performed, and results are published. For an experiment to be valid it must be repeatable and reproduce the same results.

Dr. J. B. Rhine founded the Duke University Parapsychology Laboratory in 1930. Parapsychology was taken from the German usage by J. B. Rhine to describe the stringently experimental approach to study psychic phenomenon. His work on the subject achieved worldwide recognition. He also created the Foundation for Research on the Nature of Man (FRNM). The laboratory is still highly sought for a degree in Parapsychology.

Early beginnings

The interest in paranormal or supernatural events have been around for centuries. The catholic church investigated demon possessions, alchemist in the Middle Ages performed experiments that could be considered parapsychological. John Dee a mathematician, astronomer, and astrologer in the mid-1500s, performed experiments using a divining rod and pendulum to find lost objects (Broughton, 1991).

Franz Anton Mesmer while studying at the University of Vienna in the 1760s, developed a theory that the moon, sun, and stars influenced all organized bodies "through the medium of subtle fluid, which pervades the universe, and associates all things together in mutual intercourse and harmony." His experiments led to using mineral magnets as treatment for healing. He called the effect on the healer (himself) "animal magnetism" he would use sweeping motions of his hands and other gestures. Those who experienced his mineral healing would often lose control of their limbs, convulse, or slip into a trance, all part of the healing process. (Broughton, 1991)

The term mesmerize was from Mesmer's treatments. Today mesmerism is called hypnotism. Initially, parapsychologist refused to entertain ghost stories. It was against what J. B. Rhine was trying to accomplish. Being recognized as a legitimate science. Through the years, the term has extended past the boundaries J. B. Rhine set. The ghost sightings, apparitions, and other bizarre occurrences are now grouped under parapsychology.

Early physical researchers believed the investigations of poltergeist, apparitions, and ghost could provide evidence we have souls or independently existing consciousness that is separate from the body and indeed even survives the death of body. For some parapsychologists search for evidence remains important and have brought to parapsychology investigations into reincarnation and a variety of quasi-experimental attempts to answer what, if anything, survives bodily death (Broughton, 1991).

Spiritualism

Emmanuel Swedenborg was credited as starting a movement with his teachings of communicating with spirits. Swedenborg's followers used mesmeric trance to communicate with spirits. The mesmerists

believed the "higher phenomena" such as clairvoyance, thought transference, etc., were natural occurrences with no connection to the spiritual. (Broughton, 1991)

What Parapsychology Is Not

Here are a few topics parapsychology does not support. Astrology, the investigation of UFOs (UFOlogists usually investigates), and strange, unidentified creatures such as Bigfoot, the Loch Ness Monster, etc.

What is studied

Parapsychology involves the study of a variety of proposed psychic phenomena by scientists and scholars, including the search for evidence of their existence. Among these phenomena are:

- *Precognition*: perceiving information from the future, such as in a vision or dream

- *Clairvoyance*: perceiving information about distant locations

- *Telepathy*: communicating mind-to-mind (without the use of normal senses)

- *Extrasensory perception (ESP)*: perception that seems to transcend the five senses, encompassing the above terms

- *Psychokinesis* or *telekinesis*: manipulating objects with the power of the mind

- *Out-of-body experiences (OBEs)* (such as perceiving one's own

body from above)

- *Apparitions and hauntings*

What is psi?
Psi is a general term used in parapsychology for the phenomena studied by the field, including cognitive one such as mind-to-mind communication as well as physical ones such as the movement of an object with one's mind.

What are paranormal phenomena? Parapsychology: Fact and Fiction
Critics of parapsychology cite a lack of robust evidence of true paranormal activity and difficulty repeating apparent findings. They also argue that parapsychologists have not been able to rule out all natural explanations for the phenomena they study. (Psychology Today, 2021)

While historical demonstrations and notions about psychic phenomena have often been shown to be false, contemporary parapsychologists have sought to use the scientific method to test their hypotheses with empirical evidence. Nevertheless, even some of the most high-profile research into apparent psychic phenomena has been challenged due to methodological concerns. (Psychology Today, 2021) Did psychologists find proof of ESP?

In 2011, a major psychology journal published a paper that reported evidence for precognition—including seemingly impossible

phenomena like study participants being more likely to "recall" words that they only studied after the fact. However, other scientists struggled to replicate these findings, and some critics suggest the original studies exemplify how insufficiently careful methods can produce misleading results. (Psychology Today, 2021) Should I read into coincidences?

Coincidences can be startling and thought-provoking—the term "synchronicity" has been used to describe seemingly meaningful events with no apparent cause-and-effect link—there are reasons to be skeptical about coincidences reflecting something supernatural. These include people's tendencies to seek patterns and tell coherent stories about potentially random occurrences. (Psychology Today, 2021)

Criminology is the study of why individuals commit crimes and why they behave in certain situations. By understanding why, a person commits a crime, one can develop ways to control crime or rehabilitate the criminal. There are many theories in criminology. Some attribute crimes to the individual; they believe that an individual weighs the pros and cons and makes a conscious choice whether to commit a

crime. Others believe it is the community's responsibility to ensure that their citizens do not commit crime by offering them a safe and secure place in which to live. Some ascertain that some individuals have latent traits that will determine how they will react when put in certain negative conditions. By studying these theories and applying them to individuals, perhaps psychologists can deter criminals from repeating crimes and help in their rehabilitation. (Criminology.com, 2021)

Choice Theory: The belief that individuals choose to commit a crime, looking at the opportunities before them, weighing the benefit versus the punishment, and deciding whether to proceed or not.

Classical Theory: Like the choice theory, this theory ascertains that people think before they proceed with criminal actions; that when one commits a crime, it is because the individual decided that it was advantageous to commit the crime.

Conflict Theory: The conflict theory holds that crime results from the conflicts in society among the different social classes, and that laws arise from necessity because of conflict, rather than a consensus.

Critical Theory: Critical theory upholds the belief that a small few, the elite of the society, decide laws and the definition of crime; those who commit crimes disagree with the laws that were created to keep control of them.

Labeling Theory: Those who follow the labeling theory of criminology ascribe to the fact that an individual will become what he is labeled or

what others expect him to become; the danger comes from calling a crime a crime and a criminal a criminal.

Life Course Theory: The theory that a person's "course" in life is determined by short (transitory) and long (trajectory) events in his life, and crime can result when a transitory event causes stress in a person's life causing him to commit a crime against society.

Positivist Theory: The positivist rejects the idea that everyone makes a conscious, rational choice to commit a crime; rather, some individuals are abnormal in intelligence, social acceptance, or some other way, and that causes them to commit crime.

Rational Choice Theory: Reasons that an individual thinks through each action, deciding on whether it would be worth the risk of committing a crime to reap the benefits of that crime, whether the goal be financial, pleasure, or some other beneficial result.

Routine activity theory: Followers of the routine activity theory believe that crime is inevitable, and that if the target is attractive enough, crime will happen; effective measures must be in place to deter crime from happening.

Social Control Theory: Theorists believe it is society's responsibility
to maintain a certain degree of stability and certainly in an individual's life, to make the rules and responsibilities clear, and to create other activities to thwart criminal activity.

Social disorganization theory: Suggests that crime occurs in communities that experience breakdown in social mores and opportunities, such as in highly populated, lower income, urban communities.

Social Learning Theory: Social learning indicates that individuals learn from those around them; they base their morals and activities on what they see others in their social environment doing.

Strain Theory: The theory holds that individuals will turn to a life of crime when they are strained, or when they are unable to achieve the
goals of the society, whether power, finance, or some other desirable goal.

Trait Theory: Those who follow the trait theory believe that individuals have certain traits that will contribute to whether they can commit a crime when pushed in a certain direction, or when they are in duress.

<h1 style="text-align:center">Index of characters and films</h1>

DSM-5 Manual APA (2013)

Clinician's Thesaurus 8th Edition Edward L. Zuckerman (2019)
Encyclopedia Horrifica Joshua Gee (2007)

Life magazine Explores Inside the Criminal Mind Understanding How Bad People Think (2021)

Life magazine The Most Notorious in American History (2008)

Parapsychology The Controversial Science Richard S. Broughton, Ph.D. (1991)

Understanding Mental Disorders, your guide to DSM-5 by APA (2015)

World's Creepiest Abandoned Places Haunted, Mysterious,

Frightening Centennial Legends magazine (2020)

https://sawfilms.fandom.com/wiki/John_Kramer
https://houseandhistory.com/amityville-horror-house/
https://villains.fandom.com/wiki/Sebastian_Caine
https://avp.fandom.com/wiki/Alien_vs._Predator_(film)
https://avp.fandom.com/wiki/Alan_%22Dutch%22_Schaefer

https://avp.fandom.com/wiki/Royce   https://avp.fandom.com/wiki/Isabelle

https://hellraiser.fandom.com/wiki/Lament_Configuration
https://**www.psychologytoday.com/us/basics/parapsychology**[1]
https://**www.criminology.com/understanding-criminology-theories/**[2]

---

1. http://www.psychologytoday.com/us/basics/parapsychology

2. http://www.criminology.com/understanding-criminology-theories/

Excerpt from
Psychology of...Horror Villains, Survivors, and
Victims. Movie Edition Volume II
Section 1
Vampirism

Vampirism has been around for centuries all over the world there are tales of creatures who shape shift and drink blood. Clinically, vampirism comes in various forms:

- Autovampirism is drinking your own blood.
- Vampirism is drinking the blood of others.
- Necrophagia is eating the flesh of others.
- Necrophilia is sexual excitement and having contact with corpses.
- Necrosadism is the abuse of corpses.
- Cannibalism is eating other humans.
- All these are termed "Renfield's Syndrome" introduced by clinical psychologist Richard Noll. He used the character R. M. Renfield from Bram Stoker's novel *Dracula* (1897).

Clinical vampirism can vary in how frequent or intense a person is. For some it is only occasional. Others become paranoid, display schizophrenia, aggressive, and violent behavior towards others (Guiley, 2005).

Before Bram Stoker gave us the pinnacle version of the vampire Dracula, John Polidori published *The Vampyre* (1819). Both Polidori and Stoker created a new version of who and what the vampire was. Vampires were dangerous, repulsive Demons. Depending on the country, vampires go by different names such as *Strigoi/Shtriga (Albania), Vrykolakas (Greece), Empusae (Greece), Lamiae (Greece), Moroi (Romania), Guaxa (Spain), Soucouyant (Trinidad), Tunda/Patasola (Colombia), Loogaroo (Caribbean), Obayifo (West Africa),* and *Rakshasas (India)* believed to be where the vampire myth began.

The earliest recorded tale of human blood suckers was in 1734, *The Travels of Three English Gentlemen* (Redfern, 2017). The vampire folklore spread by word of mouth. The vampire could shift into various animals, mist, and could increase his size. Vampires were not beautiful, alluring, charming, and wealthy like our movies and tv shows portray.

My analysis of Dracula will include comparison and contrast of how he is portrayed through different decades. How our view of the vampire has evolved or devolved in some cases.

*"The Order of the Dracul, the Dragon. An ancient society, pledging my forefathers to defend the church against all enemies of Christ. Their relationship was not entirely...successful-*Dracula to Johnathan Harker

Bram Stoker's Dracula 1992

Count Dracula

Background

Vlad Dracul was a warrior for the Catholic church. He was a good man, faithful to his wife, faithful to the church.

Inciting Event:

In 1496 while battling the Turks, his wife received a note telling her Vlad had died in battle. She became distraught with grief and took her life by jumping from the tower window. When Vlad returned, he found his wife dead with the priest. As he cried out in pain from her death, the priest told him her soul was damned and she would not see Heaven.

This enraged Vlad. He gave his life to the church, but his wife will be forsaken by the church and the God he served. Vlad renounces his vow to God and then stabs the cross causing it to bleed. In his anger, Vlad proclaims to avenge his wife's death. He drinks the blood from the cross and claims blood is life. This action condemns him to live as an immortal being needing blood to survive. Without blood he ages, and his strength is diminished.

Murders:

Vlad had caused thousands of deaths as a templar. Known for impaling his enemies. As Dracula he killed thousands more over the centuries.

Psychological aspect:

Vlad gave all his loyalty to the church and to his wife. The feeling of betrayal set off his breakdown. The intense rage he felt is common when a person has been betrayed. Vlad experienced a traumatic event, and his anger fueled his acts of violence.

Could Vlad have been helped?

There was no way to change the outcome. Vlad was coming back from battle tired, mentally drained, emotionally unstable. To see his wife's lifeless body put him in turmoil. The priest making the comment of his wife's spiritual damnation is what caused Vlad's descent. If the priest would have comforted Vlad instead of condemning, grieving could have begun and the path to healing from such a traumatic incident.

Volume II coming soon!

Don't miss out!

Visit the website below and you can sign up to receive emails whenever S. L. Yarbrough publishes a new book. There's no charge and no obligation.

https://books2read.com/r/B-A-ZQUQ-CEJTB

BOOKS2READ

Connecting independent readers to independent writers.